PRAISE FOR
Passing It On

In a time when families are often pulled in different directions and during an age when the family dinner table seems to fade into the background gathering dust, *Passing It On* gives voice to God's call for us to live in community with one another—gathering together to hear and reflect on the stories of the Christian faith. This book provides a tool for families as they seek ways to pass on the faith from generation to generation. With intentional and faithful discipline, Oliver provides a means for bringing the family back together. Gathered together, families are invited to live into the seasons of the Christian year, pay attention to God's presence in their lives, and discuss and share their experiences with the Holy.

—Rev. Dr. Tanya Marie Eustace
Director of Children and Intergenerational Ministries
Discipleship Ministries of The United Methodist Church

Seek intention in a world of divided attention! While the marketplace skips ahead, selling next season's wares before this one even starts, this book will help families live more deeply by practicing presence in the present moment. Whatever your family looks like, wherever you live, *Passing It On* makes room for you to foster and record your shared wisdom intergenerationally. There is room here for preschoolers, grandparents, teens, stepparents, siblings, family members close at hand, and a world of beauty yearning to be engaged. As a practical theologian, I thank Oliver for this invitation into practicing the formation that is already happening with more engagement, encouragement, and delight.

—Dr. Melinda McGarrah Sharp
Assistant Professor of Pastoral Theology and Ethics
Phillips Theological Seminary, Tulsa, Oklahoma
Author of *Misunderstanding Stories: Toward a Postcolonial Pastoral Theology*

Kara Lassen Oliver has offered us an amazing guide that allows families to grow in faith together throughout the calendar and Christian year. Drawing from ancient patterns of prayer, scripture, and a child's need for ritual, this resource will strengthen the connection among parents, children, and God.

—Melanie C. Gordon
Director of Ministry with Children
Discipleship Ministries of The United Methodist Church

PASSING IT ON

How to Nurture Your Children's
Faith Season by Season

KARA LASSEN OLIVER

UPPER
ROOM BOOKS®
NASHVILLE

Cover design: Left Coast Design, Portland, Oregon
Cover photo: © Vinogradov Illya / Shutterstock.com

LIBRARY OF CONGRESS CATALOGING-IN-PUBLICATION DATA

Oliver, Kara.
  Passing it on : how to nurture your children's faith season by season /
Kara Lassen Oliver.
      pages cm
  Includes bibliographical references.
    ISBN 978-0-8358-1497-3 (print)—ISBN 978-0-8358-1498-0 (ebook)—ISBN 978-0-8358-1536-0 (mobi)
  1. Christian education of children. 2. Seasons—Religious aspects—Christianity. I. Title.
  BV1475.3.O45 2015
  248.8'45—dc23   2014047969

Printed in the United States of America

To

Claire Marin and Carter

who daily prompt me to slow down,
look for God,
and love bigger than I knew was possible

CONTENTS

INTRODUCTION

In our family's first condo the laundry was located in the basement of our unit. Family members had to go out the front door, around the corner, and down a dozen wide concrete steps to get there. Navigating this simple path with laundry on one hip and a two-year-old's tiny hand in the other always invited adventure. One day as Claire and I rounded the corner and made our way to the eighth step, I saw a small garter snake sunning itself in our path.

The sight startled me, programmed as I am with some ancient distrust of this slithering creature. But the enlightened, theologically educated woman in me knew instantly that I did not want to pass on my irrational fear of such a little and harmless creature. So after a quick intake of breath I exclaimed to my innocent daughter, "Look, Claire, God made snakes too." I hoped that the high pitch of my voice landed on her ears, full of delight at God's wonderful creation and not as the choked anxiety of a mother wanting desperately to do the right thing.

That moment remains a touchstone for me as the time I realized that I not only made sure Claire ate her vegetables, modeled good manners, and learned her numbers and colors; I was also forming her worldview, her perspective on creation, and her first images of God. The seed for this book was planted that day.

I knew then that I wanted to pass on my faith to my daughter (and later my son) in an explicit way but without being so heavy-handed and dogmatic that they would reject tradition, ritual, and scripture outright. I grasped in that moment on the step that I wanted to pass on more than Bible stories, scripture verses, and beautiful hymns. I wanted to pass on a delight in God's good creation, a freedom to question and wonder, a responsibility to think deeply about how to live as Jesus would live, and a playfulness that would allow for the in-breaking of the Holy Spirit.

That initial desire has entailed my practicing daily an awareness of life and finding the courage to be present in each moment. I have had to practice silence, kneel at the altar for Communion, pick up pen and journal, discipline myself to pray, explore the labyrinth, fast, and give myself to Bible study. I wanted to introduce my children to the spiritual practices that will help them meet God, come to know Jesus, and recognize the work of the Holy Spirit in their lives.

As families—parents, grandparents, trusted adults—we shape our children. We form them as football fans, musicians, athletes, consumers, readers, environmentalists, and so on. We hold strong opinions about what age children should drink soft drinks, how much TV and electronics they may consume, which books they should read. We give great thought to forming our children in body and mind.

Barely four years old, my nephew stands in his candy-cane-striped athletic pants chanting, "Hoo hoo, Hoosiers." His parents did not agonize over whether or not he would be a Hoosier fan. They did not drill him to memorize the fight song. They have intentionally, successfully, and joyfully formed a lifelong Indiana University sports fan by spending time together watching games and singing the fight song.

Formation comes as a function of time, practice, and symbol. Some families are forming sports fans. Some are spending lots of time outside hiking and biking, practicing habits of recycling. We form our families by the ways we spend our time, our regular habits, and the symbols that repeat themselves on our clothing and refrigerator magnets.

Yet *choosing* to form our children spiritually seems more intimidating, more difficult and abstract. For many parents, spiritual formation sounds like a burden, an impossibility, a task for which they feel unqualified. But the same practices that form a die-hard Hoosier or a politically astute child—family time, regular practice, and concrete symbols—can convey Christian tradition and spirituality to our children with equal joy and lasting effect. As we engage in spiritually forming one another, family members spend time together with God, develop spiritual practices, and incorporate Christian symbols into our lives. We can read Bible stories, name the squirrels and butterflies—and snakes—as God's good creation, and take a moment to pray for those sleeping in the cold tonight.

I offer ideas on how to give the same time, attention, and book learnin' to forming our children spiritually that we give to forming them in other ways. Four weeks per season I will invite you to look daily for God's presence and activity in your life and the lives of your children. Each week offers a simple liturgy, or process, for leading discussion with your family members about where they saw and experienced God as well as for learning about the spiritual practice for the coming week.

I encourage you to join other parents in a Sunday school class, Wednesday night church setting, or neighborhood group of your own making to talk about the joys and challenges of parenting and bravely choosing to embark on this journey of spiritual formation. Read the Letter of Encouragement to Parents. Be gentle with yourself. Offer grace to your partner and the other parents in the small group. Trust that God is at work. What you plant in one season may not take root and flower for many seasons to come, but God honors the efforts and the desires of your heart.

Also take time to explore the website oliverkml.wordpress.com, which will provide downloads of the weekly symbols, examples of unique ways to explore the practices, and stories to help illustrate the weekly themes for children of different ages. With your help and participation we will build a catalog of images, books, movies, and activities that help all parents pass it on!

USING THIS RESOURCE

When I worked as a youth pastor, I invited a counselor from a local youth shelter to speak at a parent meeting. She provided a lot of helpful information, but one piece of advice has stuck with me. She advised that families begin having family meetings when children are young and when the questions, rules, and issues are simple. "Because," she said, "when you really need the family meetings to agree on curfews, schedule activities, and settle disagreements on family chores and consequences, it's too late to convince your teenager of the benefits of family meetings." I would add to the counselor's advice that family meetings foster the spiritual practice of community, prayer, and formation. If you and your children can begin praying together, talking about experiences and questions about God, and creating intentional time to listen to joys and heartbreaks when they are young, then you establish a firm foundation for when they enter puberty and teenage years. The weekly gatherings outlined for each week of four key seasons of the year are designed to help families create that safe place within the week for parents and children to listen to one another, listen for God, and prayerfully follow the promptings of the Holy Spirit in the world.

The academic world will dictate the amount of time spent on weekly activities and assignments. Sports and music lessons will demand daily and weekly practice. And children already memorize the meaning and values of symbols that bombard them on television, radio, electronic devices, and T-shirts. Our children are being formed. This weekly gathering gives your family time to practice the disciplines of the Christian tradition and learn together the symbols of our faith so that you intentionally participate in the spiritual formation of your children.

CREATING A SUCCESSFUL FAMILY GATHERING

Choose a regular and consistent time for your Family Gathering.
Some families may prefer to start their week on a Sunday evening. Some may prefer Saturday morning as a review of the week. Others may choose a Wednesday evening to keep weekends free. Experiment with different times to discover best availability and times when everyone feels fresh, but settle into this routine as soon as you can.

Keep the Family Gathering to one hour.
The Family Gathering may take only twenty minutes, depending on what has happened in your family's life that week, as well as the number of questions, joys, and prayer concerns. Be sure that you don't extend beyond one hour. You and your children will feel better about committing to meeting if you know what to expect. If you have younger children, you may need to limit the meeting to thirty minutes.

Questions, concerns, or topics that require more attention probably will come up during the Family Gathering: an item to talk with a teacher about, an unresolved issue between siblings, a scheduling conflict. Make note of these matters, promise to talk about them, and agree on a day and time to address each issue. Avoid dealing with prolonged specifics, planning, or discussion during the Family Gathering. Keep your time together focused.

Choose a quiet and comfortable space.

Make sure everyone has space to sit comfortably, whether you gather around the kitchen table or lounge on couches and chairs in the living space. And be sure that TVs, phones, and other electronic distractions (cell phones) are turned off or removed from the room. It's important that each family member has the full attention of everyone else.

Have needed supplies ready and in the space.

Choose a drawer in the room or a small box to place in the room that contains Bible(s), this book, pens or markers. The website offers varied ways to open and close your time; some may require a candle and matches or other supplies.

DESIGN AND FLOW OF THE FAMILY GATHERINGS

Different family members are encouraged to lead the Family Gathering each week, unless it specifies an adult. And you may also ask that various members lead different parts each week. The leader will guide the family through each movement of the gathering, reading the prayers and asking for responses. The prayers and sections that appear in bold for the leader serve as suggested wording only. As you begin Family Gatherings, it may be more comfortable for one of the parents to lead the time together. Leading in this setting does require the ability to read.

The design of the Family Gathering remains the same each week so that everyone becomes familiar with the pattern and flow. In time, even the youngest among your family could ask what everyone is thankful for, ask someone to read the scripture, and lead the Lord's Prayer. The parts of the Gathering are as follows:

- The Opening for the first week of the season sets the context for the coming weeks. In the remaining weeks of the season, the Opening involves a simple prayer that recognizes God and names the practice of the previous week. The leader will pray the prayer aloud or ask everyone to read the prayer together. Then the leader invites each person to name one or more things for which he or she gives thanks for from the week, such as a good grade, a pet, a special person, the rain, or a beautiful song.

- The Word gives time to read scripture related to the symbol and the practice of the week. The leader may read the scripture aloud, ask for a volunteer, or invite family members to read it in unison. The verse is printed in the book for ease, but the leader may suggest that each person bring a Bible and find the verse. This practice encourages familiarity with the Bible by teaching the location of the various books. Reading from the Bible draws our children's attention to it as integral to our life of faith and an important symbol in our Christian tradition.

- The Response will differ each week. The interactive approach helps participants remember, explore, and delve a little deeper into their experience of the practice. The leader reads the Response ahead of time in order to feel comfortable guiding this portion of the meeting.

- The book provides blank space for one or more people to write a few words, draw a picture, or record a specific prayer or insight from the sharing. The space does not allow for a detailed or verbatim account of all responses but serves as a kind of journal or snapshot of what your family found valuable about the practice and would like to remember. When you look back on this space, you will remember what you have passed on to your children.

- The Looking Forward prepares everyone for the coming week. The leader will read the description of the symbol and the practice. The symbol, a simple and common visual, reminds each person to remember God during the week. The practice is named aptly because the truth at the heart of this book is that forming ourselves as disciples of Jesus requires intention, repetition . . . practice. Make sure everyone understands how he or she will practice paying attention to God this week. A specific daily practice is listed for persons according to age and developmental stage. Allow time for each person to read his or her practice; read and explain to smaller children. These are options and suggestions. Your family may choose to practice the same option or a junior high (grades 5–8) may want to try the practice described for the senior high (grades 9–12). The assignments are not rigid. The goal is an awareness of God every day. When everyone understands his or her daily practice, read together the full scripture reference for the week. The single printed verse offers convenience, but I encourage you to read the entire passage from the Bible.

- The Closing Prayer gives family members the opportunity to mention persons, situations, and places in need of prayer, such as college decisions, those recovering from natural disasters, a sick friend, a soccer game. After all have named their prayer requests, the leader will offer a short prayer and then the whole family will pray together the Lord's Prayer.

Before dispersing, decide who will lead the next Family Gathering. Deciding who leads each week also teaches our children whom we value as leaders—women and men, children and adults. We are all children of God with gifts and abilities to lead.

Parent Reflection Groups

I encourage you to participate in a parent reflection group. As a youth pastor I was struck by how surprised and delighted parents were to hear that other parents wrestled with similar developmental, disciplinary, and relational issues. Parenting requires herculean effort. After long hours of work, grocery shopping, filling out school forms, and carpool duty, it's easy to judge ourselves and assume that every other household manages better than ours. In the reflection groups, parents discover that many struggles are universal. They also hear what has worked well for some families and what has absolutely failed for others.

Beyond the daily struggles of keeping your child healthy and in shoes that fit, you seek a community of parents that understands your deep desire to pass along your faith to your child. While you can talk with your colleague at work about when to start piano lessons or swap recipes with your neighbor, you also need a community that values prayer, desires formation in the likeness of God, and longs to model a Christlike life.

Talk with your pastor about helping you organize a parent reflection group; ask if anyone in your Sunday school class would like to join you and your family in a four-week commitment. If you do not have a church home, send an e-mail to friends whom you trust and who you know have similar longings and desires for their children.

There is value in meeting with parents who have children the same age as yours, but there is also richness in meeting with families who have children at various ages and life stages. Don't feel confined to create a group for preschool families or parents of teenagers.

These reflection groups of your peers will help you extend grace to your children, be more forgiving of yourself, and find creative and new ways to pass on your faith to your children. You will find a weekly guide for these reflection groups on pages 59–76.

THE VALUE OF DAILY CHECK-INS

Our children were nearly three and nine when my husband, Jeff, and I started experimenting with a new ritual at dinnertime called "sads, glads, and sorries." After serving the food and offering a prayer, Jeff and I would go around the table and ask each person, "What made you happy today?" And we would hear about insects on the sidewalk, playing a game with a friend, or a good day at work. Then another round, "What made you sad today?" And my daughter might mention a friend who missed school because he was sick; my son might tell us about a broken toy; and I might refer to a news story that made me sad.

Finally, each family member would answer the question, "Is there anything you need to say you are sorry for?" When we first began this tradition, my toddler son, Carter, preferred to tell what *the rest of us* should say we're sorry for: "Claire, you should say you're sorry for locking me out of your room." "Daddy, you need to say sorry for putting me in time out." We would giggle and apologize for the log of grievances that Carter had been keeping for the day. I came to realize the powerful effect on our children of my apologizing to my husband in front of them or the effect on us as parents hearing our daughter apologize for ignoring her brother when she had a friend over.

This simple and brief ritual gave us all enough time to remember our day, share the highs and lows, and reconcile in meaningful ways regardless of age. And the tradition has continued for years. Often our younger child prompts us to begin. As my husband and I flop into our chairs after busy days, while our adolescent daughter is consumed with homework, waiting to get back to her phone, Carter will ask, "What made you happy today?" And his question brings us into the present moment, causes us to look up from our plates into one another's eyes, and perhaps connect for the first time that day.

Along with the Family Gatherings described earlier, I suggest that parents check in with their kids each day. Most parents do this naturally and multiple times a day. As parents we ask our kids how they slept, what is happening at school that day, how the day was, and tuck them in at night. Daily check-ins like "sads, glads and sorries" remind us to listen to our children with God's ears and see them through God's eyes. This check-in is separate from—and in addition to—daily practice for parents and caregivers. Unlike the process for establishing Family Gatherings, you need not agree upon a time, manner, and place for it. Committing to daily check-ins expresses your prayerful decision to ask, listen, and pray for your child every day.

You may choose to sit with your child every morning at breakfast. It may mean getting up early to pack lunches so that you can sit at the table while she eats her oatmeal and ask her how she is, how she can enter into the daily practice today, and tell her you are praying for her.

You may decide to be home every night for dinner so that you can sit together and hear about your son's day, ask if he saw or remembered the weekly symbol anywhere in his day, and tell him about your day.

Or you and your spouse may decide to put your kids to bed at night as a twosome, to sit at the foot of the bed and tell stories about the day, sit on the floor after reading bedtime stories and enjoy a minute of silence, or kneel together to say your prayers.

The many ways to check-in are as varied as the families reading these words. And you don't need to tell your child, "I'm going to check in with you now." Simply ask God to give you eyes of grace and ears of love and offer your child your undivided attention every day. The goal is to talk, listen, pray, and remember the daily prayers and practices together.

THE LORD'S PRAYER

(for use in all weekly sessions)

Our Father, who art in heaven,
hallowed be thy name.
Thy kingdom come,
thy will be done on earth as it is in heaven.
Give us this day our daily bread.
And forgive us our trespasses,
as we forgive those who trespass against us.
And lead us not into temptation,
but deliver us from evil.
For thine is the kingdom, and the power, and the glory,
forever. Amen.

LETTER OF ENCOURAGEMENT TO PARENTS

Don't let anyone look down on you because you are young. Instead, set an example for the believers through your speech, behavior, love, faith, and by being sexually pure.

—1 Timothy 4:12

When I first heard the words printed above, they gave me great hope. I was in high school when our youth pastor asked members of the youth group to memorize this verse. But I had already experienced a community of adults that allowed me to trust the truth of these words so that I could live my faith with confidence even as a young person. My supportive, generous, and wise parents introduced me to my first spiritual disciplines with a lit candle and prayers. When I received my Bible at confirmation, my pastor inscribed it with the words, "Don't stop asking good questions. And don't be satisfied with half-baked answers." When I expressed an interest in ministry, I was invited to serve as a liturgist in the much larger church my family attended when I was in high school. Our youth leader encouraged us to take responsibility for our faith: to study scripture, pray regularly, be of service to our community, and treat everyone with kindness and love. I felt fortunate that no one looked down on me because of my youth but encouraged me to try to be faithful—to speak and act with love, to ask for forgiveness when I failed, and to receive God's grace that encouraged me to try again.

As a parent I want my children to grow up with that same loving, generous, and forgiving community of adults. When I put my son to bed, I tell him, "God loves you." He responds, "God loves you too." I view him as necessary to my formation as I am to his. When I have tried on three outfits for a night out and my daughter struts into my bedroom to roll her eyes at my vanity, it reminds me that God has gifted me with a wise teacher.

Parents, do not look down upon your children because they are young but let them set an example for you. Invite them into the activities in this book with gentleness and the expectation that you will teach and learn from one another. Your toddler may not sit still for a single Family Gathering, and when you ask her what she is thankful for she may say "cows" every week. And that's okay. Your elementary school child may bounce up and down the whole time or inject potty words into every prayer (if your son is like mine) and it doesn't mean you should abandon your efforts. Your teenager may snarl and insist on having her cell phone within reach of every gathering. He may refuse to answer any questions or even make eye contact for the entire four-week series. That is okay too.

Tell your children honestly and vulnerably why you desire that they have a relationship with God, know the stories of Jesus, and recognize the voice of the Holy Spirit. Model for them your willingness to try these practices each day and week even when it's awkward. Be clear about your expectations. Don't allow them to be disrespectful. But pray and trust that if you spend time together, encourage them to practice their faith, and teach them the symbols of the faith, God will work in their lives, drawing them closer.

You will know my children intimately after reading all the stories in this book, but indulge me in one more. . . .

When Claire was four years old I took her with my youth group to a Taizé worship service (a worship service based on the Taizé monastic community in France, which includes sung and chanted prayers, meditation, silence, and scripture readings). This particular night a labyrinth was laid out on the floor, and everyone was encouraged to walk the labyrinth during the service. (A labyrinth is a single path to the center, or heart, of God walked prayerfully for spiritual formation). Several of the youth entered the labyrinth and began to walk. Claire and I stepped up to the labyrinth; I stood behind her and placed my hands on her shoulders, directing her along the path. She kept shaking off my hands, walking faster, and trying to get away from me. The more I struggled to keep her on the path, the more she insisted on veering over the lines and into others' paths. Finally, I just let her go.

Claire selected one of the youth already walking and followed behind her. She walked step for step behind this young woman until they reached the heart of God. They sat in silence briefly and then followed the single path back out.

I had taken Claire to the worship service and had explained the purpose of the labyrinth. But she found the heart of God on her own. She chose the pace and her traveling companion. I could simply watch and pray and give thanks.

Parents, do not look down on yourselves because you are young parents. Instead, set an example for your children through your speech, behavior, love, and faith.

Go in peace!

Advent

Preparing to Receive the Gifts of Christmas

My family had the privilege of serving as United Methodist Volunteers in Mission in the small African nation of Malawi from 2009–2011. Our son, Carter, was just three years old at the time but already quite stubborn. And from day one he informed us that he would not learn any Chichewa, the native language of the people where we lived. True to his word, he greeted people only in English and refused to repeat the names of basic items like *madzi* (water) or *galu* (dog).

When our family boarded a plane ten months later for a visit in Nashville, Tennessee, he began singing a chorus that we had sung in church nearly every Sunday. As he buckled his seat belt and the plane taxied down the runway, he sang in perfect pitch and rhythm and pronunciation *in Chichewa*. Jeff and I looked at each other in wonder. I nearly started to cry as I understood that despite his protests, he had been listening and memorizing. The words and tune had sunk in and become a part of him. We tickled him and he giggled, delighted that he had surprised us and thrilled by his mischief.

So it no longer surprises me that every Advent now eight-year-old Carter refuses to admit that he knows the names of the characters in the Nativity scene. What is Jesus' mother's name? Blank stare. "Who is this guy?" I ask, holding the carved figure with a sheep around his shoulders. "I don't know," he says with a twinkle in his eyes. We have bought age-appropriate Nativity sets—fabric ones he could throw without breaking, plastic ones large enough not to be choking hazards, handcrafted ones from toilet paper tubes to engage his interest. But every Advent, he refuses to admit that he recognizes the characters, knows their names or the story line.

Despite Carter's obstinacy, Jeff and I continue to spend time in worship, recite the story and sing the hymns, and display the Nativity scenes around the house. I know that one day while sitting on a plane or in a school cafeteria or a cubicle at work, Carter will tell the story. The time, practice, and symbols in our home are not wasted. He is listening, memorizing, and understanding.

The season of Advent, which leads to the secular celebration of Christmas, provides an excellent opportunity to consider the spiritual formation of our children while offering time to practice spiritual disciplines together. We are familiar with the four seasons of the year: winter, spring, summer, and fall. But the church year also celebrates various seasons. Advent begins the Christian year and includes the four Sundays before Christmas (December 25). Advent has its roots in the Latin word *adventus*, or "coming." This season proclaims the coming of Christ in the birth of Jesus that we celebrate on Christmas Day. Our task during Advent is to prepare for Jesus' coming.

As Christmas approaches, many parents take seriously whether their children open gifts on Christmas Eve or Christmas morning, whether Santa and his elves wrap stocking stuffers or not, what kind of Advent wreath we will get and where we will place the Nativity. And we pass on our family traditions through word and action with great enthusiasm and conviction to our children.

During the next four weeks we want to channel that same fervor and preparation in the telling of the story of Jesus' birth, the arrival of God-with-Us. The symbols and practices in the coming weeks are the gifts we receive as believers and followers of Jesus. We find ourselves reassured of the Holy Spirit's presence with us in all seasons, ages, and circumstances; we experience hope in God's presence; we emphasize prayer, our privilege and ability to communicate directly with God; and we participate in a community of faith that points to God, leads us to faith, supports us through difficult seasons of life, and celebrates with us.

When the much anticipated day of Christmas arrives, along with the presents under the tree, your children will have already received the gifts of God's presence, everlasting hope, prayer, and the love of community.

Advent Week 1: Presence

Intro to Advent and Family Gathering

Opening

Once everyone finds a comfortable seat, an adult or other family member can begin by saying,

Just like the year has four seasons—winter, spring, summer, and fall—the church also celebrates different seasons. We call the current church season Advent, and it's actually the beginning of the new year for the church. Advent means "coming" because we celebrate the coming of Jesus. On Christmas we will celebrate Jesus' birth.

Every year we busily prepare for Christmas day: the cookies and the presents and seeing our family. This year we also want to pay closer attention to God. While we bake and decorate and shop, we also want to prepare our hearts to receive Jesus on Christmas day, to remember that we are celebrating Jesus' birthday.

Our task during Advent is to prepare for Jesus' coming.

Each week we will look for symbols in our daily life that remind us that God is with us. We will practice living the ways Jesus wants us to live.

The Word

Say, **Let's begin this week by remembering the birth of Jesus as it is told in the book of Luke in the New Testament.** Invite a member of the family to find Luke 2:1-7 in the Bible and read the verses aloud.

Looking Forward

Invite a participant to read the practice for the week. Then say, **This week our practice involves remembering that God is always with us. Just as God was present when Mary and Joseph made their long trip, when they couldn't find a place to sleep, and in the moment when Jesus was born, God is with us in boring times, difficult times, and happy times.**

Ask for a volunteer to read the description of the CIRCLE symbol. (See page 21.) Say, **Every time you see a circle this week remember that God is with you right then! Can you think of examples of where you might see circles this week?**

Then read the appropriate daily practice for each person based on his or her age. Answer any clarifying questions, or adjust as needed.

Closing Prayer

Close by asking for any joys and concerns. The leader or any family member can lead a prayer that recalls these specific requests. Close by praying the Lord's Prayer together. If this prayer is new for your family, you may copy the prayer from this book (page 15) or write it on a sheet of paper so that everyone can see it and pray it aloud together.

PRESENCE: "The fact or state of being present; position close to a person." God is with us in this moment now, and we can share it with God.

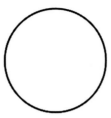

The CIRCLE reminds us that God has no beginning and no end. God has always been and will always be with us.

Read Luke 2:1-7.

> **[Mary] gave birth to her firstborn child, a son, wrapped him snugly, and laid him in a manger, because there was no place for them in the guestroom (v. 7).**

DAILY PRACTICE

Every time you see a circle today (a ponytail holder, a tire, the letter *O*), remember in that moment that God is with you.

Toddler & Elementary	Every time you see a circle today say, "God is with me."
Junior & Senior High	Every time you see a circle today imagine what God is seeing and feeling right where you are. What does God see on your drive to school? How does God feel walking through your school? What does God want you to notice about your family?
Adult	What does it mean that God is always with you? that God is always with your children—even when you can't be? How does that knowledge affect or change your prayers for your child(ren)?

DAILY PRAYER

Post this prayer where it is easily seen—on your front door or the bathroom door, the refrigerator, a car dashboard, or on the dining room table. Pray the prayer throughout the day, individually and together.

> ***Dear God, I want to see you in every moment today. Amen.***

Family Gathering

(after a week of practicing Presence)

Opening

Dear God, last week we looked for you every day in every part of our lives. Thank you for . . . [each person may offer thanks for pets, people, answered prayers, weather, events, grades, safety, birthdays, and so on].

The Word

[Mary] gave birth to her firstborn child, a son, wrapped him snugly, and laid him in a manger, because there was no place for them in the guestroom (Luke 2:7).

Response

Ask each person to think back over the week and remember something that brought happiness. Then recall something that brought sadness. If family members feel comfortable, each person can speak them aloud.

Draw or write in the journaling space below something that describes where family members felt God during both the good and the bad of the week.

Looking Forward

Read the definition of HOPE and the description of the STAR in Advent Week 2. Have little ones trace the shape with their finger and remind everyone to look for the symbol this week.

Then have each person read (if able) his or her daily practice. Discuss any questions, and feel free to make modifications.

Turn in your Bibles, and read together Matthew 2:1-2.

Closing Prayer

Dear God, today we pray for . . . [each person may name people, situations, events, concerns that they need prayer for this week].

Pray together the Lord's Prayer.

ADVENT WEEK 2: HOPE

HOPE: "Desire accompanied by expectation of fulfillment." (The faith that God is always working for good in the world.)

The STAR reminds us of the hope of the wise men. When they saw the star in the sky they believed it signaled God's work of doing a new and good thing. Their hope gave them courage to make a long journey to see with their own eyes the work of God.

Read Matthew 2:1-2.

[The magi] asked, "Where is the newborn king of the Jews? We've seen his star in the east, and we've come to honor him" (v. 2).

DAILY PRACTICE

Every time you see a star shape today let it remind you of the wise men who hoped to find the Christ child and of your hope.

Toddler & Elementary	Each day tell an adult you love what you hope for. For example, "Today I hope we get to go to the playground."
Junior & Senior High	Remember something good that has happened in the past. What does that experience make you hope for in the future?
Adult	What is your greatest hope for your children? Tell your children each day what you hope for them.

DAILY PRAYER

You may post this prayer on your door, the refrigerator, your dashboard, or on the dining room table. Pray the prayer throughout the day, individually and together.

Dear God, when life is difficult, shine your light of hope. Amen.

Family Gathering

(after a week of practicing Hope)

Opening

Dear God, this past week we remembered your star in Bethlehem and looked for hope in our own lives. Thank you for . . . [each person may offer thanks for pets, people, answered prayers, weather, events, grades, safety, birthdays, and so on.]

The Word

[The magi] asked, "Where is the newborn king of the Jews? We've seen his star in the east, and we've come to honor him" (Matt. 2:2).

Response

Ask everyone to close their eyes; then read the scripture aloud one more time. Have each person imagine the star in the sky. Read the scripture one more time and ask each person to remember one of the stars he or she saw this week. Ask, **What emotions or thoughts about God came to your mind when you saw that star?**

Encourage family members to draw or write about their response to seeing that star.

Looking Forward

Read the definition of PRAYER and the description of the TREASURE CHEST for next week. Have little ones trace the shape of the treasure chest with their finger and remind everyone to look this week for the symbol or for items that open and close.

Then have each person read (if able) his or her daily practice. Discuss any questions, and feel free to make modifications.

Turn in your Bibles, and read together Luke 2:15-19.

Closing Prayer

Dear God, today we pray for . . . [each person may name people, situations, events, concerns that they need prayer for this week].

Pray together the Lord's Prayer.

ADVENT WEEK 3: PRAYER

PRAYER: "An address to God; an earnest request or wish." (Communication with God through thoughts, words, and gestures.)

The TREASURE CHEST reminds us that we can share our most precious thoughts with God in prayer. Your prayers are as valuable as gold, silver, and precious gems. The prayers from your heart are treasured in God's heart.

Read Luke 2:15-19.

Mary treasured all these words and pondered them in her heart (v. 19, NRSV).

DAILY PRACTICE

Every time you see a treasure chest or box today, remember that you can tell God all the thoughts you keep inside and that God will treasure them.

Toddler	Every time you open a box, remember God's love in your heart.
Elementary	Imagine your heart as a treasure chest. Tell someone what is in your heart.
Junior & Senior High	We place our most precious possessions in a treasure chest. Imagine that your heart is the chest, and tell God what is inside—happiness, sadness, compassion, jealousy.
Adult	What experiences with your children do you treasure in your heart? Tell your spouse or child(ren) one of these stories each day, and then relay to God what that experience of sharing means to you.

DAILY PRAYER

You may post this prayer on your door, the refrigerator, your dashboard, or on the dining room table. Pray the prayer throughout the day, individually and together.

Dear God, listen to all the love and feelings I treasure in my heart. Amen.

Family Gathering

(after practicing a week of Prayer)

Opening

Dear God, last week we remembered Mary's love for Jesus and told you what we love. Thank you for . . . [each person may offer thanks for pets, people, answered prayers, weather, events, grades, safety, birthdays, and so on.]

The Word

Mary treasured all these words and pondered them in her heart (Luke 2:19, NRSV).

Response

Draw a picture of a treasure chest in the journaling space below.

Have each person write one thing about this week that he or she never wants to forget.

Looking Forward

Read the definition of COMMUNITY OF FAITH and the description of the CIRCLE OF FRIENDS. Have little ones trace the shape with their finger and remind everyone to look for the symbol this week.

Then have each person read (if able) his or her daily practice. Discuss any questions, and feel free to make modifications.

Turn in your Bibles, and read together Luke 2:22-35.

Closing Prayer

Dear God, today we pray for . . . [each person may name people, situations, events, concerns that they need prayer for this week].

Pray together the Lord's Prayer.

ADVENT WEEK 4: COMMUNITY OF FAITH

COMMUNITY OF FAITH: A gathering of people who share God's love and with whom we share our gifts.

The CIRCLE OF FRIENDS reminds us that Christians gather together around God.

Read Luke 2:22-35.

Led by the Spirit, [Simeon] went into the temple area. Meanwhile, Jesus' parents brought the child to the temple so that they could do what was customary under the Law. Simeon took Jesus in his arms and praised God (vv. 27-28).

DAILY PRACTICE

This week give thanks for the people in your community of faith.

Toddler & Elementary	Hug or high-five or shake hands with people this week that you want to be in your circle of friends—maybe your grandparents, friends at school, your sister or brother, neighbor.
Junior & Senior High	Think about the people in your life whom you trust, admire, feel safe talking to and asking questions of. Imagine them in your circle of friends. Consider writing them a short note thanking them for being part of your community of faith.
Adult	Who has formed your faith, helped you understand God, supported you? Whom do you want to be part of your child(ren)'s life? Invite them over for dinner or ask them to reach out to your child(ren).

DAILY PRAYER

You may post this prayer on your door, the refrigerator, your dashboard, or on the dining room table. Pray the prayer throughout the day, individually and together.

Dear God, I am grateful for my circle of friends who love you. Amen.

Family Gathering

(after a week of practicing Community of Faith)

Opening

Dear God, last week we gave thanks for the people who love us and pray with us. Thank you for . . . [each person may offer thanks for pets, people, answered prayers, weather, events, grades, safety, birthdays, and so on.]

The Word

Led by the Spirit, [Simeon] went into the temple area. Meanwhile, Jesus' parents brought the child to the temple so that they could do what was customary under the Law. Simeon took Jesus in his arms and praised God (Luke 2:27-28).

Response

Ask each member to speak about a person in his or her circle of friends. Don't ask questions or contradict. Simply listen to the characteristics that make this person special.

Ask each person to write a word or phrase that describes the friend or draw a picture of him or her.

Closing Prayer

Dear God, today we pray for . . . [each person may name people, situations, events, concerns that he or she needs prayer for this week].

Pray together the Lord's Prayer.

LENT

Living in the Awkward Season

When our daughter, Claire, decided she wanted to continue the Oliver family tradition and become the fourth generation to attend the boarding school that her father, uncle, grandfather, and great-grandfather had attended, our family faced challenges. Preparing ourselves emotionally, physically, spiritually—and financially—for this commitment was daunting.

During Claire's application process for admission, scholarships, and financial aid, many people prayed with our family and supported us along the way. As the time for a decision approached, Claire's enthusiasm and desire to attend the school grew, but Jeff's and my confidence about affordability did not grow at the same rate. We shared our anxiety and concern with friends and family. And one day we received a message from dear friends in Malawi, where we used to live, telling us that they were fasting and praying for Claire's admission and adequate financial aid. Their sacrifice and devotion humbled us. Telling Claire about their commitment and prayers on her behalf made real for us in a new way the power and relevance of spiritual practices. Their act of devotion comforted Claire, Jeff, and me more than anything else during our waiting and discernment.

Author Pam Hawkins refers to Lent as the "awkward season." It's a church season that starts on a Wednesday (Ash Wednesday) rather than on a Sunday like most Christian seasons and holidays. The season of Lent consists of the forty days prior to Easter, not including Sundays. And while the journey of Lent leads to the great good news of resurrection celebrated on Easter Sunday, many Christians (Protestant and Catholic) begin somberly with ashes on foreheads that remind us of our mortality. During an Ash Wednesday service, ashes (often left from burned Palm branches of the previous Palm Sunday) are placed on each person's forehead in the shape of a cross with the words, "Remember that you are dust, and to dust you shall return." Easter comes with a bright and hopeful proclamation that life and light always conquer death and darkness. But during Lent, Christians have traditionally practiced three serious and sacrificial disciplines—prayer, fasting and almsgiving—that draw us closer to God and help us understand the disciplines and sacrifices that marked Jesus' life, especially during his last days. Lent is indeed an awkward season and can be difficult to explain to children.

Prayer, fasting, and charity may already be regular habits in your home. If so, the season of Lent and the daily practices offered here provide the opportunity to talk about their deep roots in the life and story of Jesus and their power and efficacy today. If these are unfamiliar practices, I invite you to step into them—however awkward they may feel. God will meet you there and draw you forward to the celebration of Easter.

Lent Week 1: Repentance

Intro to Lent and Family Gathering

Opening

Once everyone is seated comfortably, one of the adults can begin by saying, **As we begin to think about spring and new life blooming in nature, the church is also preparing to celebrate new life. This is the season of Lent when we remember the life and death of Jesus so that on Easter we can joyfully celebrate Jesus' new life through his resurrection.**

Lent is the time when we remember that Jesus faced temptations to turn away from God and that we also face temptations every day. The temptation to sin, to make decisions that hurt us or hurt other people, is real. During Lent we remember that Jesus chose to love God all day, every day, and to love all people even when they behaved in mean or unfair ways. During Lent we remember that Jesus believed that God's love and faithfulness was the most powerful force in the world.

This Lent we will practice choosing to love as Jesus chose to love God. Each week we will look for symbols in our daily life that remind us that God wants us to love ourselves, one another, and God.

The Word

Say, **We start this week by admitting that we don't always act the way God desires. Sometimes we fight instead of using kind words. Sometimes we lie instead of telling the truth. Sometimes we are selfish instead of generous. The first step on the road to Easter comes in repenting, which means we say we are sorry and try to be loving again.** Invite a member of the family to find Daniel 9:3-6 in the Bible and read it aloud.

Looking Forward

Ask someone to volunteer to read the practice for the week. Say, **This week our practice is repentance, admitting when we do something wrong and trying to make it right. Sometimes we pray. Sometimes we apologize. Sometimes we ask for a "do-over."**

Have a volunteer read the description of the symbol. Use the explanation of ashes in the introduction if your family needs more details. Say, **This week, every time you see ashes or dust or track dirt into the house, ask yourself if there is something you need to say you are sorry for. Remember that God loves you no matter what and wants all God's people to forgive and love one another.**

Then, read the appropriate daily practice for each person based on his or her age. Answer any clarifying questions, or adjust as needed.

Closing Prayer

Close by asking for any joys and concerns. The leader or any family member can lead a prayer that recalls these specific requests. Close by praying the Lord's Prayer (page 15) together.

REPENTANCE: "Feel[ing] sorrow for one's sin and mak[ing] up one's mind to do what is right."

Over forty passages in the Bible associate ASHES with mourning and grief. Throughout the Old Testament and continuing to today, ashes represent an outward sign of inward repentance.

Read Daniel 9:3-6.

> **I then turned my face to my Lord God, asking for an answer with prayer and pleading, and with fasting, mourning clothes, and ashes. As I prayed to the LORD my God, I made [my] confession (vv. 3-4).**

DAILY PRACTICE

Choose what is right, even if it is difficult or scary.

Toddler	When you do something wrong this week, remember that an apology can wipe it away like ashes can be wiped away.
Elementary	When you make a bad decision, apologize and imagine ashes being blown away. Then make a good decision.
Junior High	We all make mistakes. When you make a mistake this week, tell someone, apologize, and do what you can to make it right.
Senior High	Think about decisions you have made or are making that require your repentance. Talk with a trusted adult about how to choose what is right.
Adult	When you have the opportunity, explicitly tell your child about a time when you made a bad decision, apologized, and made a different choice. Try to tell that story in the midst of the day, perhaps when you've lost your temper while driving, let a curse word slip, or gossiped.

DAILY PRAYER

You may post this prayer on your door, the refrigerator, your dashboard, or on the dining room table. Pray the prayer throughout the day, individually and together.

> ***Dear God, give us the courage to admit when we are wrong. Amen.***

FAMILY GATHERING

(after practicing a week of Repentance)

OPENING

Dear God, we have felt sorry for our bad decisions, and we always want to turn back to you because you love us forever. Thank you for . . . [each person may offer thanks for pets, people, answered prayers, weather, events, grades, safety, birthdays, and so on.]

THE WORD

Change your hearts and lives! Turn back to God so that your sins may be wiped away (Acts 3:19).

RESPONSE

Ask participants to think back over the week and remember something that made them happy during the week. And then ask that they remember something that made them sad.

Invite family members to draw or write something in the journaling space below about where they sensed God's presence during both the good and the bad of the week.

LOOKING FORWARD

Read the definition of FASTING and the description of the EMPTY PLATE. Have little ones trace the shape with their finger and remind everyone to look for the symbol this week.

Then ask each person to read (if able) his or her daily practice. Discuss any questions, and feel free to make modifications.

Turn in your Bibles, and read together Exodus 34:28.

CLOSING PRAYER

Dear God, today we pray for . . . [each person may name people, situations, events, concerns for which he or she needs prayer this week].

Pray together the Lord's Prayer.

LENT WEEK 2: FASTING

FASTING: "To eat no food for a period of time." (Traditionally, not taking food or drink or both for a spiritual purpose and for a set period of time. Fasting can include giving up any activity that draws our attention away from God [video games, texting, TV] and replacing it with prayer.)

The EMPTY PLATE reminds us that we depend on God. We eat food that makes us healthy. We also need to feed on scripture, prayer, and acts of kindness every day to have a healthy relationship with God.

Read Exodus 34:28.

> **[Moses] was there with the LORD forty days and forty nights. He didn't eat any bread or drink any water. He wrote on the tablets the words of the covenant, the [Ten Commandments].**

DAILY PRACTICE

Take some time each day to praise God for providing what you need.

Toddler	After eating say, "Thank you, God, for food."
Elementary	Set the table for your family this week, and pray a prayer with every plate you put on the table.
Junior High	When you receive a plate of food or wash or put away the dishes, remember that God created the earth that provides all we need for life.
Senior High	Consider fasting from one or more meals this week and using that time to pray about a decision you need to make. Trust that God will provide what you need—physically and otherwise.
Adult	We often skip meals because of a busy schedule. But deliberately fast during one or more meals this week and dedicate that time to prayer. Tell your children about it.

DAILY PRAYER

You may post this prayer on your door, the refrigerator, your dashboard, or on the dining room table. Pray the prayer throughout the day, individually and together.

Dear God, I know that I need you as much as I need food. Amen.

Family Gathering

(after practicing a week of Fasting)

Opening

Dear God, thank you for all you provide. Our prayer is to work with you so that everyone has enough. Thank you for . . . [each person may offer thanks for pets, people, answered prayers, weather, events, grades, safety, birthdays, and so on.]

The Word

Jesus said, "When you fast, don't put on a sad face like the hypocrites. They distort their faces so people will know they are fasting. I assure you that they have their reward" (Matt. 6:16).

Response

Ask everybody to close their eyes and imagine persons who draw attention to themselves when they fast as someone reads Matthew 6:16-18 aloud. Read the scripture one more time, and ask each person to imagine persons who fast quietly, giving attention to God instead of others. Ask family members to record one thing they learned about fasting

Looking Forward

Read the definition of CHARITY and the description of the LOAF OF BREAD. Have little ones trace the shape with their finger and remind everyone to look for the symbol this week.

Then have each person read (if able) his or her daily practice. Discuss any questions, and feel free to make modifications.

Turn in your Bibles, and read together Luke 12:33.

Closing Prayer

Dear God, today we pray for . . . [each person may name people, situations, events, concerns that he or she needs prayer for this week].

Pray together the Lord's Prayer.

Lent Week 3: Charity

CHARITY: "The act of giving money, food, or other kinds of help to people who are poor, sick, etc." (Generosity and helpfulness toward those who are needy or suffering.)

The LOAF OF BREAD reminds us that we often read about Jesus taking, breaking, and sharing bread with those who are hungry.

Read Luke 12:33.

> Jesus said, "Sell your possessions and give to those in need. Make for yourselves wallets that don't wear out—a treasure in heaven that never runs out. No thief comes near there, and no moth destroys."

DAILY PRACTICE

Be generous and helpful.

Toddler	Every time you eat bread, offer a piece to someone else.
Elementary	Every time you eat bread, remember children in your city and around the world who do not have enough to eat.
Junior & Senior High	Be generous with friends and strangers this week. Offer the best that you have—not just your leftovers.
Adult	Choose a family, organization, or local charity, and make a contribution as a family. If possible, go together to give your donation.

DAILY PRAYER

You may post this prayer on your door, the refrigerator, your dashboard, or on the dining room table. Pray the prayer throughout the day, individually and together.

Dear God, give me a generous heart. Amen.

Family Gathering

(after practicing a week of Charity)

Opening

Dear God, thank you for those who have shared what they have with me. Help me to be generous with what I have. Thank you for . . . [each person may offer thanks for pets, people, answered prayers, weather, events, grades, safety, birthdays, and so on.]

The Word

Jesus said, "Sell your possessions and give to those in need. Make for yourselves wallets that don't wear out—a treasure in heaven that never runs out. No thief comes near there, and no moth destroys" (Luke 12:33).

Response

Ask each person to tell a story of one thing he or she gave or received this week. What did family members learn about charity?

Draw pictures of those things.

Looking Forward

Read the definition of DEVOTION and the description of the PALM BRANCH. Have little ones trace the shape with their finger and remind everyone to look for the symbol this week. Then have each person read (if able) his or her daily practice. Discuss any questions, and feel free to make modifications.

Turn in your Bibles, and read together Matthew 21:8-9.

Closing Prayer

Dear God, today we pray for . . . [each person may name people, situations, events, concerns that he or she needs prayer for this week].

Pray together the Lord's Prayer.

Lent Week 4: Devotion

DEVOTION: "Prayer, worship, or other religious activities that are done in private rather than in a religious service." (Devotion can happen anywhere you experience God.)

The PALM BRANCH symbolizes goodness and victory. When Jesus arrived in Jerusalem, the people shouted and celebrated his arrival right there in the road. They didn't have to be in the right building or have the right candles or books. They cut palm branches and waved them like flags. They didn't go buy a fancy carpet; they spread their cloaks on the ground.

Read Matthew 21:8-9.

> **Now a large crowd spread their clothes on the road. Others cut palm branches off the trees and spread them on the road. The crowds in front of [Jesus] and behind him shouted, "*Hosanna* to the Son of David! *Blessings on the one who comes in the name of the Lord! Hosanna* in the highest!"**

Daily Practice

Choose a time during each day to praise God for God's goodness and to ask God for help.

Toddler	When you see leaves waving in the wind, say thank-you to God out loud.
Elementary	Let the trees remind you that you can pray any time. Pray a prayer each time you see leaves waving in the wind.
Junior & Senior High	You don't have to limit praising God and praying to Sunday mornings. Choose a time and place other than Sunday at church when you will give thanks to God each day.
Adult	Make daily prayer—praise and petition—your devotion this week.

Daily Prayer

You may post this prayer on your door, the refrigerator, your dashboard, or on the dining room table. Pray the prayer throughout the day, individually and together.

Dear God, I want to praise you every day. Amen.

Family Gathering

(after practicing a week of Devotion)

Opening

Dear God, we know that you want to talk with us every day. Call to us and listen to us. Thank you for . . . [each person may offer thanks for pets, people, answered prayers, weather, events, grades, safety, birthdays, and so on.]

The Word

Now a large crowd spread their clothes on the road. Others cut palm branches off the trees and spread them on the road. The crowds in front of [Jesus] and behind him shouted, "*Hosanna* to the Son of David! *Blessings on the one who comes in the name of the Lord! Hosanna* in the highest!" (Matt. 21:8-9).

Response

Draw a picture of a palm branch in the journaling space below.

Have each person write or draw one way he or she worshiped God this week.

Closing Prayer

Dear God, today we pray for . . . [each person may name people, situations, events, concerns that he or she needs prayer for this week].

Pray together the Lord's Prayer.

SUMMER

Turning Ordinary into Extraordinary

One summer my daughter and I attended SoulFeast, a spiritual formation event hosted by The Upper Room. Five-year-old Claire participated in the daily activities for the kids while I attended Bible study, workshops, and worship. One night that week as she got ready for bed she started telling me the story of a boy who asked his dad for money. When he got the money, he went and wasted it all. He had to go work with the pigs and their slop.

I smiled to myself, engaged by her earnest storytelling, and asked questions drawing out the rest of the story. She told me that the boy decided to go home and tell his dad that he had wasted the money. "What did his dad do?" I asked incredulously. "He gave him the best clothes and the best food, and they had a party," she said very matter-of-factly.

"You know," I said, thrilled at the teachable moment, my ability to recognize it, and my presence of mind to engage Claire in this wonderful dialogue, "that story is in the Bible." Without missing a beat, she replied, "I know, Mom. It's a parable."

Argh! Totally deflated and having to laugh at myself, I simply acknowledged that yes, it was indeed a parable. What more could I do but lean against the sink while she continued to educate me between brushing and swishing by telling me two more parables she had learned.

The summer months can create simultaneous relief from the rigid schedules and looming tasks and deadlines of the school year while also providing endless hours to fill with fun and creativity. Some of us have the freedom to turn off morning alarms, let the kids lounge, and make trips to the park and the pool. Others continue with full-time jobs, childcare, or camps. Hopefully everyone enjoys some freedom in these months whether it is Vacation Bible School at your local church or time to sit in lawn chairs and tell stories—parables and otherwise.

The church calendar refers to this season of the church year as Ordinary Time. A longer season than Advent or Lent, this season focuses on the big picture. The scriptures during Ordinary Time tell us the story of redemption: God working since the day of creation in partnership with humanity, God coming in the person of Jesus, and God promising ultimate redemption of all created things. In these coming weeks I encourage you to focus on creation, creativity, and beauty! You pursue this focus not because you have to produce something for a grade, not so your project gets extra credit for creativity, or to add another activity to that college application. You choose this focus because the world we live in and each of us were created by an imaginative and loving God who delights in color, beauty, music, and movement. These ordinary summer days can become extraordinary when we recognize God's presence in every moment—early morning snuggles, blocks piled high on the floor, sidewalk chalk, and bike rides in the neighborhood.

Take time in the coming days and weeks to notice, point to, and create beauty with your family. We can form our children into lovers of creation, cocreators of beauty, stewards of this good earth, and persons who seek the redemption of the world.

Summer Week 1: Art

Intro to Summer and Family Gathering

Opening

Once everyone is seated comfortably, one of the adults can begin by saying, **Summer is here! And you may be worried or even upset that we are sitting here as a family to talk about what we are going to do this summer. You are probably glad that school is out, and you don't have to worry about assignments and deadlines for a while. Well, you can relax. In the next four weeks we are not going to give you reading assignments or worksheets or term papers. We just want you to look for beauty—to see God in nature, art, bubbles in the bathtub, and the moon in the sky.**

At school you sit for long hours, don't get to be outside as much as you'd like, and do more listening than doing. This summer we want you to see, create, and enjoy beauty. We want you to hear, move, write, and understand that God created us to use our gifts to make the world a more beautiful, kind, and just place for all.

The Word

Say, **We start this week by reminding ourselves that God has given each of us the ability to create. And clearly God thinks beauty is an important part of the world and our lives.** Invite a family member to find Exodus 35:30-35 in the Bible and read it aloud.

Looking Forward

Have a volunteer read the practice for the week. Say, **This week we want to take time to let our minds slow down, to let our brains relax, and to put tests and reading assignments and schedules behind us as much as we can. This week we will look for and create art. Nature often inspires art. It also inspires us to create art of our own. Ask God what artistic gifts you have to create beauty. If you are three or thirteen, get out some paper and finger paints. Help your parents plant flowers. Look for art and dare to create some yourself!**

Have a volunteer read the description of the symbol. Talk about how wonderful it is that God values art and beauty. You may want to choose a special place in your home where family members can display their art for everyone to see.

Then read the appropriate daily practice for each person based on his or her age. Answer any clarifying questions, or adjust as needed.

Closing Prayer

Close by asking for any joys and concerns. The leader or any family member can lead a prayer that recalls these specific requests and close by praying the Lord's Prayer together. If this prayer is new for your family, you may copy the prayer from this book (page 15) or write it on a sheet of paper so that everyone can see it and read aloud together.

ART: "Something that is created with imagination and skill and that is beautiful or that expresses important ideas or feelings."

The ARK OF THE COVENANT was a beautiful chest that held the Ten Commandments, constructed with great skill by Moses as directed by God.

Read Exodus 35:30-35.

> **[Bezalel and Oholiab] have been given the skill to do every kind of work done by a gem cutter or a designer or a needleworker in blue, purple, and deep red yarns and in fine linen or a weaver or anyone else doing work or creating designs (v. 35).**

DAILY PRACTICE

Use your unique skills to make something beautiful.

Toddler	Tell someone every time you see something beautiful. Make something beautiful.
Elementary	Choose one of your talents or skills, and use it to create something beautiful.
Junior High	Art can be something useful or something to display. Create something today you think is beautiful.
Senior High	Art displays to the world what the artist thinks is important and valuable. Create something this week that expresses what you love and value.
Adult	Art is for everyone—engineer, homemaker, athlete, and teacher. What art do you love? Take time to enjoy or make art this week.

DAILY PRAYER

You may post this prayer on your door, the refrigerator, your dashboard, or on the dining room table. Pray the prayer throughout the day, individually and together.

Dear God, help me see and create beauty today. Amen.

Family Gathering

(after a week of practicing Art)

Opening

Dear God, thank you for art and beauty in the world. Thank you for . . . [each person may offer thanks for pets, people, answered prayers, weather, events, grades, safety, birthdays, and so on.]

The Word

God has made everything fitting in its time, but has also placed eternity in [human beings'] hearts, without enabling them to discover what God has done from beginning to end (Eccles. 3:11).

Response

Ask each person to think back over the week and remember something that brought happiness; then recall an event that brought sadness.

Invite family members to draw or write something in the journaling space below about how making art and looking at art show them God.

Looking Forward

Read the definition of MUSIC and the description of the LYRE. Have little ones trace the shape with their finger and remind everyone to look for the symbol this week.

Then have each person read (if able) his or her daily practice. Discuss any questions, and feel free to make modifications.

Turn in your Bibles, and read together 1 Samuel 16:23.

Closing Prayer

Dear God, today we pray for . . . [each person may name people, situations, events, concerns that he or she needs prayer for this week].

Pray together the Lord's Prayer.

SUMMER WEEK 2: MUSIC

MUSIC: "The use of skill and creativity especially in the making of things that are beautiful to look at, listen to, or read."

The LYRE is a small ten-string harp that reminds us of David and his ability to soothe with music.

Read 1 Samuel 16:23.

Whenever the evil spirit from God affected Saul, David would take the lyre and play it. Then Saul would relax and feel better, and the evil spirit would leave him alone.

DAILY PRACTICE

Add music to your life.

Toddler & Elementary	Sing every day! Sing your favorite song or make up a new one.
Junior & Senior High	Listen to a different radio station, explore your siblings' or parents' music library. Listen to as many kinds of music as you can. Which music does God use to speak to you?
Adult	What music soothes you? Intentionally choose music that gives you joy—good lyrics, brilliant instrumentals. Let music be God speaking to you this week.

DAILY PRAYER

You may post this prayer on your door, the refrigerator, your dashboard, or on the dining room table. Pray the prayer throughout the day, individually and together.

Dear God, delight me with music. Amen.

FAMILY GATHERING

(after a week of practicing Music)

OPENING

Dear God, thank you for musicians who dedicate their gifts and lives to notes and lyrics and song. Thank you for . . . [each person may offer thanks for pets, people, answered prayers, weather, events, grades, safety, birthdays, and so on.]

THE WORD

Praise the Lord!

. . . .

Praise God with drum and dance!
  Praise God with strings and pipe!
Praise God with loud cymbals! . . .
Let every living thing praise the Lord!
Praise the Lord! (Psalm 150:1, 4-6).

RESPONSE

Ask those present to close their eyes, and then read the scripture again. As they listen, ask them to imagine all the instruments and music. Read the scripture one more time, and ask each person to imagine the kind of music he or she would like to play.

Encourage family members to note some lyrics that reveal God to them or to draw a picture in the space provided of where they would like to play music.

LOOKING FORWARD

Read the definition of DANCE and the description of the TAMBOURINE. Have little ones trace the shape with their finger, and remind everyone to look for the symbol or for items that open or close this week.

Then have each person read (if able) his or her daily practice. Discuss any questions, and feel free to make modifications.

Turn in your Bibles, and read together Exodus 15:20.

CLOSING PRAYER

Dear God, today we pray for . . . [each person may name people, situations, events, concerns that he or she needs prayer for this week].

Pray together the Lord's Prayer.

SUMMER WEEK 3: DANCE

DANCE: "A series of rhythmic and patterned bodily movements usually performed to music."

The TAMBOURINE with metal disks only makes music when someone moves and shakes it, reminding us that we can celebrate and praise God with our own movement.

Read Exodus 15:20.

Then the prophet Miriam, Aaron's sister, took a tambourine in her hand. All the women followed her playing tambourines and dancing.

DAILY PRACTICE

Dance! Dance in any way you can—tap your toes, bob your head, shake your whole body.

Toddler	Instead of walking, dance everywhere!
Elementary	Dance today—by yourself or with a friend, to the radio or with a tambourine, inside or outside, serious or silly, in front of a mirror or with your eyes closed.
Junior & Senior High	Dance today in thanksgiving to God; move your body to music! By yourself or with a friend, to the radio or with a tambourine, inside or outside, slow or fast, serious or silly, in front of a mirror or with your eyes closed.
Adult	We can praise God with our bodies by dancing. Tap your foot while you do dishes, invite your spouse or child to dance in the living room. Boogie in the yard or slow dance in your bedroom.

DAILY PRAYER

You may post this prayer on your door, the refrigerator, your dashboard, or on the dining room table. Pray the prayer throughout the day, individually and together.

*Dear God, thank you for fingers and toes and legs and arms
that can move and dance. Amen.*

FAMILY GATHERING

(after practicing a week of Dance)

OPENING

Dear God, thank you for the reminder that we can worship you with our whole bodies. Thank you for . . . [each person may offer thanks for pets, people, answered prayers, weather, events, grades, safety, birthdays, and so on.]

THE WORD

**A time for crying and a time for laughing,
a time for mourning and a time for dancing (Eccles. 3:4).**

RESPONSE

Ask each person to tell the family about how dancing makes him or her feel—free or embarrassed, joyful or self-conscious. Don't ask questions or contradict. Simply listen.

Draw a picture of a tambourine in the journaling space below. Have each person write on or around the tambourine a word that describes how dancing makes him or her feel.

LOOKING FORWARD

Read the definition of WRITING and the description of the PEN. Have little ones trace the shape with their finger and remind everyone to look for the symbol this week.

Then have each person read (if able) his or her daily practice. Discuss any questions, and feel free to make modifications.

Turn in your Bibles, and read together Jeremiah 30:2.

CLOSING PRAYER

Dear God, today we pray for . . . [each person may name people, situations, events, concerns that he or she needs prayer for this week].

Pray together the Lord's Prayer.

SUMMER WEEK 4: WRITING

WRITING: "To form letters or words on a surface with an instrument (as a pen or pencil); to form the letters or the words of." (To put down ideas, thoughts on paper.)

The PEN reminds us of the importance of capturing stories, truth, and wisdom on paper.

Read Jeremiah 30:2.

The Lord, the God of Israel, proclaims: Write down in a scroll all the words I have spoken to you (Jer. 30:2).

DAILY PRACTICE

Write down our thoughts—whatever they are.

Toddler	Carry a crayon, pencil, or pen and paper with you everywhere so you can write.
Elementary	Carry a pen and small notebook or scratch paper with you all day and write down ideas, lists, poems, prayers whenever they come to you.
Junior & Senior High	Write a journal entry every day. Record the events of the day, how they made you feel, a prayer. Write a few sentences or a few pages.
Adult	Each day write about a time, place, or relationship where you felt God's presence or absence.

DAILY PRAYER

You may post this prayer on your door, the refrigerator, your dashboard, or on the dining room table. Pray the prayer throughout the day, individually and together.

Dear God, thank you for all the people who have written so that I can know and learn. Amen.

Family Gathering

(after practicing a week of Writing)

Opening

Dear God, remind me to write so that I don't forget what I have learned. Thank you for ... [each person may offer thanks for pets, people, answered prayers, weather, events, grades, safety, birthdays, and so on.]

The Word

Go now, write it before them on a tablet, and inscribe it in a book, so that it may be for the time to come as a witness forever (Isa. 30:7).

Response

Ask each member of the family to read something he or she wrote this week. For the young ones, it may be a picture. Each person could read one sentence or an entire short story. Make one affirming comment on each piece shared.

Write in the space below the words, *Thank you, God, for words that record our story.* Invite each person to write all or part of their writing in the space below.

Closing Prayer

Dear God, today we pray for ... [each person may name people, situations, events, concerns that he or she needs prayer for this week].

BACK TO SCHOOL

Growing Fruit of the Spirit

One day Jeff and I picked Carter up from preschool and as we left, Gareth, one of his friends, turned to me and said in a most accusing voice, "Carter pushed me today on the playground." And he watched to see if I would chastise or beat Carter right then and there.

Gareth and Carter have had a love-hate relationship since they met their first day of nursery school, and I knew his mother agreed when she turned back and responded with a sigh, "I'm sure he did nothing to provoke it." (nod, nod, wink, wink)

Carter has no qualms telling stories about himself—even when incriminating—so I asked, "Hey man, what happened on the playground?" And the story goes like this . . .

Watipa, a girl in his class, had gotten a haircut the day before, and she feared that the boys would laugh at her because she was "bald like a boy." She didn't want to take her hat off on the playground. Gareth kept chasing her and trying to steal her hat. So Carter concluded, "I had to block him."

Gallant, admirable, sweet boy. But still . . . Jeff and I continued to ask a few more clarifying questions, to which Carter sighed the sigh of a man often unjustly accused and concluded, "Are you really so surprised?"

As our kids return to school, we hope they reflect our example and values in their interactions with teachers and friends. We long to see them extend kindness to the new girl at school, be gentle with the boy who got the last out on the playground, and practice self-control when the hours inside seem long and the school work tedious. We celebrate the moments that peace reigns between siblings and praise God when goodness wins over mischief in the classroom.

We recognize the fruit of the Spirit in love, peace, patience, kindness, gentleness, goodness, and faithfulness in ourselves and in our children. While forming our children involves boundaries, discipline, and consequences, it also means paying attention to the work of the Holy Spirit in their lives, inspiring them to be kind and prompting them to slow down and make good decisions.

In the coming weeks, we introduce our children to some fruit of the Spirit, the marks of discipleship that point to their maturing in the faith and God at work in their lives. Through time, practice, and symbol we encourage our children to be prayerful in their everyday lives, listening for God's still small voice, living according to the example of Christ, and trusting the prompting of the Holy Spirit in all their interactions.

And, hopefully, you won't doubt your child like I did when he or she displays love, kindness, patience, and self-control.

Back to School Week 1: Love

Intro to Back to School and Family Gathering

Opening

Once everyone is seated comfortably, one of the adults can begin by saying, **It's time to go back to school. We all have mixed feelings about that. What are some things you are looking forward to about going back to school?** [*allow time for answers*] **Why aren't you looking forward to going back to school?** [*allow time for answers*]

One way that we can enjoy each day—the good and the bad—is by looking for God in each moment. In the next few weeks we will look at some of what the apostle Paul calls "fruit of the Spirit": love, patience, self-control, and kindness. If we are prayerful and pay attention to the Holy Spirit in our lives, we receive the fruit of the Spirit. This fruit blooms when we treat others well and make life—even school—better for everyone.

The Word

Say, **We start this week with a reminder that God loves us—when we are kind and when we are grumpy, when we are helpful and when we are selfish. This week we will try to love our family members and people at school at all times too.** Invite a member of the family to find 1 John 4:7 in the Bible and read the verse aloud.

Looking Forward

Have a volunteer read the practice for the week. Say, **This week we are going to make a decision to be loving. And hope that God makes it easier and easier. Remember when you had to be reminded to wash your hands? And reminded over and over again? Now you wash your hands without even thinking about it. We can choose to be loving until it comes naturally, without even thinking about it.**

Have a volunteer read the description of the symbol.

Then read the appropriate daily practice for each person based on his or her age. Answer any clarifying questions, or adjust as needed.

Closing Prayer

Close by asking for any joys and concerns. The leader or any family member can lead a prayer that recalls these specific requests and close by praying the Lord's Prayer together. If this prayer is new for your family, you may copy the prayer from this book (page 15) or write it on a sheet of paper so that everyone can see it and read aloud together.

LOVE: "A quality or feeling of strong or constant affection for and dedication to another." Love involves "the laying down of our lives in the service of God and others" (DCSF, 175).

The HEART represents the core of our being that receives, holds, and gives love.

Read 1 John 4:7.

Dear friends, let's love each other, because love is from God, and everyone who loves is born from God and knows God.

DAILY PRACTICE

This week choose to love in situations where you may not feel loving.

Toddler & Elementary	When you get angry or grumpy this week touch your heart and try to love the person you are upset with in that moment.
Junior & Senior High	Notice your heartbeat this week—faster when you see a person you like or when you feel nervous, slower when you are comfortable and relaxed. What happens to your heartbeat when you choose to love someone—a friend, enemy, teacher, sibling?
Adult	This week name (out loud or in writing to your spouse or friend) those people or situations where you find it difficult to express or feel love. Imagine your heart filled with God's love and choose to love that person or in that situation this week.

DAILY PRAYER

You may post this prayer on your door, the refrigerator, your dashboard, or on the dining room table. Pray the prayer throughout the day, individually and together.

Dear God, give me the courage to show love and the grace to accept love. Amen.

FAMILY GATHERING

(after practicing a week of Love)

OPENING

Dear God, this week we tried to choose love even when we didn't feel love. Thank you for . . . [each person may offer thanks for pets, people, answered prayers, weather, events, grades, safety, birthdays, and so on.]

THE WORD

This is how we know love: Jesus laid down his life for us, and we ought to lay down our lives for our brothers and sisters. But if a person has material possessions and sees a brother or sister in need and that person doesn't care—how can the love of God remain in him? Little children, let's not love with words or speech but with action and truth (1 John 3:16-18).

RESPONSE

Ask each person to think back over the week and remember something that made him or her happy and sad.

Draw or write something in the journaling space below about where you felt God during both the good and the bad of the week.

LOOKING FORWARD

Read the definition of PATIENCE and the description of the TURTLE. Have little ones trace the shape with their finger and remind everyone to look for the symbol this week.

Then have each person read (if able) his or her daily practice. Discuss any questions, and feel free to make modifications.

Turn in your Bibles, and read together Romans 12:12.

CLOSING PRAYER

Dear God, today we pray for . . . [each person may name people, situations, events, concerns that he or she needs prayer for this week].

Pray together the Lord's Prayer.

BACK TO SCHOOL WEEK 2: PATIENCE

PATIENCE : "The capacity to bear pains or trials calmly or without complaint."

The TURTLE moves slowly, more slowly than most animals. Traditionally thought of as wise, the turtle lives a long life.

Read Romans 12:12:

Be happy in your hope, stand your ground when you're in trouble, and devote yourselves to prayer.

DAILY PRACTICE

This week try to wait with calm and grace.

Toddler	Every time you have to wait this week, pretend you are a turtle moving very slowly.
Elementary	Try not to get frustrated when you wait this week—when you raise your hand in class, wait in line for the water fountain, wait for your parent to get groceries. Imagine yourself as a turtle moving slowly and remaining calm.
Junior High	Think about the times you find it most difficult to be patient: when talking with your parents, listening in class, taking care of a young sibling. Say a prayer during those situations, take a deep breath, slow down like a turtle.
Senior High	Often patience requires us to slow down, pay attention, and see God in the midst of our frustration. When you get impatient ask God what God would you like you to see in that moment.
Adult	Our children need to learn patience at school and understand that we can't meet all their needs immediately. We also need to slow down and see their impatience as a desire for our attention. Practice patience this week by giving attention to those who need it.

DAILY PRAYER

You may post this prayer on your door, the refrigerator, your dashboard, or on the dining room table. Pray the prayer throughout the day, individually and together.

Dear God, slow me down enough to teach me wisdom and help me see joy. Amen.

Family Gathering

(after practicing a week of Patience)

Opening

Dear God, this week we tried to be patient by slowing down and looking for you when we were frustrated. Thank you for . . . [each person may offer thanks for pets, people, answered prayers, weather, events, grades, safety, birthdays, and so on.]

The Word

Be happy in your hope, stand your ground when you're in trouble, and devote yourselves to prayer (Rom. 12:12).

Response

Ask everyone to close his or her eyes while you read the scripture one more time. Have each person imagine happy and praying people. Read the scripture one more time and ask each person to remember when he or she had to be patient or were in trouble this week.

Ask family members to draw or write about being patient when they weren't happy.

Looking Forward

Read the definition of SELF-CONTROL and the description of the YIELD SIGN. Have little ones trace the shape with their finger and remind everyone to look for the symbol this week.

Then have each person read (if able) his or her daily practice. Discuss any questions, and feel free to make modifications.

Turn in your Bibles, and read together Psalm 86:1.

Closing Prayer

Dear God, today we pray for . . . [each person may name people, situations, events, concerns that he or she needs prayer for this week].

Pray together the Lord's Prayer.

BACK TO SCHOOL WEEK 3: SELF-CONTROL

SELF-CONTROL: A discipline that allows you to stop doing things you want to do but that might not be in your best interest.

The YIELD SIGN reminds us to pause before making decisions, practicing self-control.

Read Psalm 86:11.

> **Teach me your way, Lord, so that I can walk in your truth.**
> **Make my heart focused only on honoring your name.**

DAILY PRACTICE

Find one way you can remember to pause and say a prayer in order to make good decisions.

Toddler	When your mom or dad says, "Yellow light," slow down. Listen.
Elementary	You aren't always with your mom and dad anymore. Sometimes you make decisions all by yourself. This week imagine a yield sign before you make a decision. See if you make better decisions when you pause first.
Junior High	Imagine that God has a remote control for your life. At what moments would God push pause to give you a minute to think about your next decision?
Senior High	Life doesn't stop completely when we need to make important decisions, so we need to learn how to put up our own yield signs. Notice those moments this week when you wish you could push the pause button and figure out ways to put up your own yield signs.
Adult	This week model ways that your children can pause, pray, and show self-control.

DAILY PRAYER

You may post this prayer on your door, the refrigerator, your dashboard, or on the dining room table. Pray the prayer throughout the day, individually and together.

> ***Dear God, when I yield, show me how to live your will. Amen.***

Family Gathering

(after practicing a week of Self-Control)

Opening

Dear God, we tried to control our bodies, minds, and tongues. Thank you for . . . [each person may offer thanks for pets, people, answered prayers, weather, events, grades, safety, birthdays, and so on.]

The Word

Be clearheaded. Keep alert. Your accuser, the devil, is on the prowl like a roaring lion, seeking someone to devour (1 Pet. 5:8).

Response

Ask each person to tell the family about a time he or she paused before making a decision. Don't ask questions or contradict. Draw a yield sign in the middle of the space. On the left write or draw how you wanted to act. On the right side write or draw how you acted differently after you paused.

Looking Forward

Read the definition of KINDNESS and the description of the SUNFLOWER. Have little ones trace the shape with their finger and remind everyone to look for the symbol this week.

Then have each person read (if able) his or her daily practice. Discuss any questions, and feel free to make modifications.

Turn in your Bibles, and read together Ephesians 4:32.

Closing Prayer

Dear God, today we pray for . . . [each person may name people, situations, events, concerns that he or she needs prayer for this week].

Pray together the Lord's Prayer.

BACK TO SCHOOL WEEK 4: KINDNESS

KINDNESS: Wanting and liking to do good and to bring happiness to others.

The bright and colorful SUNFLOWER reminds us of beauty offered without asking for anything in return.

Read Ephesians 4:32.

Be kind, compassionate, and forgiving to each other, in the same way God forgave you in Christ.

DAILY PRACTICE

Offer acts of kindness as gifts this week without expecting anything in return.

Toddler & Elementary	If you had five sunflowers, whom would you give them to? Do something kind for each of those people this week. Give a hug, color a picture, be a helper, offer a compliment.
Junior & Senior High	Acts of kindness are often spontaneous and unexpected. Keep your eyes open this week for people who need the beauty of a sunflower in their lives. Help someone who drops their books; send a text message to friend you haven't seen for a long time; start the dishwasher without being asked.
Adult	Kindness begins at home. Think of your child(ren)'s favorite things, and offer those things this week. Maybe your daughter loves new markers, your son loves to shoot baskets with you, or your family hasn't had a movie night for a long time. Let go of to-do lists for a minute and offer simple kindness.

DAILY PRAYER

You may post this prayer on your door, the refrigerator, your dashboard, or on the dining room table. Pray the prayer throughout the day, individually and together.

Dear God, let my kindness shine like a sunflower. Amen.

FAMILY GATHERING

(after practicing a week of Kindness)

OPENING

Dear God, this week we tried to be kind and extend your love to those we met. Thank you for . . . [each person may offer thanks for pets, people, answered prayers, weather, events, grades, safety, birthdays, and so on.]

THE WORD

> Instead, love your enemies, do good, and lend expecting nothing in return. If you do, you will have a great reward. You will be acting the way children of the Most High act, for he is kind to ungrateful and wicked people (Luke 6:35).

RESPONSE

Draw a picture of a sunflower in the journaling space below. Have each person write one kind thing that happened this week on a petal of the sunflower.

CLOSING PRAYER

Dear God, today we pray for . . . [each person may name people, situations, events, concerns that he or she needs prayer for this week].

Pray together the Lord's Prayer.

LEADER'S GUIDE FOR PARENT REFLECTION GROUPS

The pattern and content for each of the four seasons is the same. Simply turn to the week you are leading and follow the prompts for the season you are in, such as Advent, Lent, and so on.

As you prepare to lead, take time to read the introductory material and the introduction to a specific season in order to familiarize yourself with the entire resource, logistics, and explanations. The prayers and sections that appear in bold for the leader serve as suggested wording only. Follow your promptings, keeping the session as conversational and natural as possible. Allow time for personal stories and questions but be mindful of time so that you can attend to each part of the session and finish on time.

This resource offers an optional Community Building activity in Week 1. But if the participants in the group have been together before or are continuing through each of the church seasons, feel free to omit the Community Building and spend more time in conversation and answering questions about the weekly practice, symbol, and family gathering.

I provide an optional prayer practice each week. If the group commits to an hour or more for a weekly meeting, I encourage you to try these practices that will enrich your group and build a foundation for the corresponding weekly family gathering.

Week 1

Introduction to the season and preparation for the first practice

You will need books for each participant or family and a candle and matches. Place the candle at the center of your gathering.

Opening Prayer (5 minutes)

Light the Christ candle saying, **Each week we will light the candle to remember God who is always present with us here and in the lives of our families.**

Then offer the following prayer for all seasons:

> **God, we remember that we are your beloved children, and we give you thanks for the gifts of our children. We gather because of our desire to form our children in the light of your love and the power of your Holy Spirit. Amen.**

Optional Community Building (10 minutes)

Welcome participants to the study. Tell them that this session will allow time to get to know one another a little better and to gain more information about what to expect during the coming weeks.

Introductions: Have persons introduce themselves. Give people one minute to tell something about themselves and why they have chosen to participate in this group. (If your group is large, you may need to limit this to thirty seconds per person.)

Group Guidelines: Post the words *presence, prayer, preparation, participation, confidentiality,* and *courtesy* on newsprint or a board. Mention what each means for this group (see below) and ask if folks want to add to or modify these guidelines. You may want to display reminders of your group's agreement in the meeting room each time you gather.

Presence	Attend each meeting unless serious reasons keep you away.
Prayer	Between meeting times, group members pray for one another and for the group's activities.
Preparation	Group members will make every effort to participate in the daily practices and weekly gathering, doing them as diligently as life allows.
Participation	Group members will participate honestly and openly in the session activities.
Confidentiality	What is said within the group remains in the group. Members will not discuss outside the group anything others say within the group.
Courtesy	Group members will listen to one another with respect and without interrupting or engaging in side conversations. When opinions differ, group members will not attempt to persuade another to any point of view but will listen for what God may be saying in the differences.

Ask each person or couple to turn to page 22 in their books to see a sample of the weekly journaling space below the Response section. Explain that each week one or more members are encouraged to write a few words or draw a picture to capture a learning or poignant moment from the week as a record of their family journey.

Explain that parents may want to keep a separate daily journal to record snippets of conversations with their children or partners or a meaningful scripture verse. The leader will invite participants to share these reflections but only as they feel comfortable sharing with the group. Encourage parents to respect what their children write in the journaling box. Ask their permission before sharing with the group.

PRAYER OF EXAMEN (15 MINUTES)

Explain that each week the group will begin by taking time to remember the previous week, the highs and lows, the times when God felt most present and most absent.

Say, **Each week we will remember the highs and lows of our family life using the Prayer of Examen originated by Ignatius. The examen is a daily examination of our deepest feelings and desires. Ignatius called these feelings our consolations (those that connect us with God, others, and ourselves) and desolations (those that disconnect us). He believed that God would speak to us through these feelings and desires. It's not surprising that this saint felt so strongly about the examen—this prayer practice changed him from a wild soldier to a pilgrim walking barefoot to Jerusalem.**

To begin, ask everyone to find a comfortable seat and close his or her eyes if that is most comfortable. Explain that you will ask a series of questions followed by times of silence. The questions will prompt and guide their reflection. *Allow about five minutes for the guided reflection and fifteen minutes for participants to discuss with one another.*

Imagine rewinding your life to Monday of this week and then slowly begin to move forward through the week, as if you were watching a movie of your life.

- What activities did you participate in? sports, parties, church
- Where did you go? the park, school, a friend's house, the grocery
- What happened in your home? homework, crafts, time outside, movies

  Thinking of the whole week . . .

- When did you feel most peaceful? happy? joyful?
- When did you feel tired, angry, or annoyed?
- Which moments delight you?
- Which moments repel you?

  Now remember those times of looking for God.

- Where did you feel God's presence? How did it feel?
- Where did you sense God's absence? How did that differ?

After a moment of silence invite a volunteer to tell about a moment of consolation (a connection with God) or desolation (a disconnection from God). *This is not a time to offer suggestions or compare similar situations. Simply share in a safe and supportive group where God is at work in the families gathered.*

Scripture and Tradition (10 min)

Ask participants to turn to the first page of the season where they can see the Practice, Symbol, Scripture, and Prayer on one page.

Advent

Ask a volunteer to read aloud the scripture, Luke 2:1-7.

Say, **Advent has begun, a time of waiting for the birth of Jesus. But Christmas has also started—the parties and trips to see family, the to-do lists and rush and exhaustion. Too often it feels like there still isn't room for the Holy Family and for Jesus.**

Explain that this week's goal is simply to look for God, for the space where God shows up. And hopefully we can help make that space a little bigger within our families.

Ask a volunteer to read the description of the practice for this week, Presence.

Have everyone take a deep breath and tell them, **God is present . . . now.**

Repeat two or three times.

Ask a volunteer to read the description of the symbol, the Circle. Have the group brainstorm places and spaces where they might see circles this week and point them out to their children.

Finally, pray together the daily prayer, "Dear God, I want to see you in every moment today. Amen."

Lent

Ask a volunteer to read Daniel 9:3-6.

Say, **Lent is a season of preparation, starting on Ash Wednesday and ending with the great celebration of Jesus' resurrection on Easter Sunday. This week we begin that preparation by asking our children to recognize that we make choices every day—some good and some bad. And when we make bad choices we always have the opportunity to apologize, repent, and make better decisions.**

Explain that this week's goal is to recognize when we make bad decisions and have the courage and confidence to admit our mistakes and apologize. Imagine what God can do through this practice of repentance when it starts in our families.

Ask a volunteer to read the description of the practice for this week, Repentance.

Ask members of the group to talk about what it feels like to feel "sorrow for one's sin." When have they seen that sorrow in their children? How does it feel to release the sorrow by apologizing and asking for forgiveness? How have you modeled repentance for your children?

Ask a volunteer to read the description of the symbol, the Ashes. Have the group brainstorm places and spaces where they might see ashes this week and point them out to their children.

Finally, pray together the daily prayer, "Dear God, give us the courage to admit when we are wrong. Amen."

Summer

Ask a volunteer to read Exodus 35:30-35.

Say, **Summer is here! For some of us it means long, relaxing days without alarm clocks or hard and fast schedules. For some of us it means negotiating childcare and camps because we still work full-time even when the kids have time off. Hopefully, there is a little more time around the edges for less structure and more creativity.**

Explain that this week will focus on creativity and beauty. No expectations, no right or wrong.

Ask a volunteer to read the description of the practice for this week, ART.

Ask group members to talk about opportunities their children have to experience art—painting, music, dance drama. Is this a priority in their families or a luxury, an afterthought? Where did they develop a passion or disregard for art and creativity?

Ask a volunteer to read the description of the symbol, the ARK OF THE COVENANT. Have each person in the group identify an item in their home that represents the work and beauty of skilled artists.

Finally, pray together the daily prayer, "Dear God, help me see and create beauty today. Amen."

Back to School

Ask a volunteer to read 1 John 4:7.

Say, **As our children return to school, we experience the excitement of new school supplies, seeing old friends, and a return to routine. But we also experience the anxiety of a new teacher, maybe a new school. The transition affects everyone in the family.**

Explain that this week the focus is on being loving in each circumstance and relationship. Love is a choice that can transform us and transform our situations.

Ask a volunteer to read the description of the practice for this week, LOVE. Which is easiest for you and your child—to receive, hold, or give love? Where do you see your child needing or demonstrating love?

Ask a volunteer to read the description of the symbol, HEART.

Finally, pray together the daily prayer, "Dear God, give me the courage to show love and the grace to accept love. Amen."

PREPARATION FOR THE WEEK (10 MINUTES)

Explain that each week lays the groundwork for three hopes:

1. Parents look for God in their daily lives, especially around the practice for the week.

2. Parents talk with their children daily about where both parents and children see God. Encourage parents to read about Daily Check-ins on page 14.

3. Families gather together once a week for prayer and conversation. Encourage parents to read a detailed description of the Family Gathering on pages 11–13.

Make note of the white space in the book each week, example on page 22. This space is to record thoughts and insights from the week. The toddler in the family can draw a picture; a teenager can write song lyrics. This is the journal of the family's faith journey through the seasons. If the space is not enough, encourage participants to buy a blank journal for family use.

CLOSING (5 MINUTES)

Offer a prayer of your own or something like this, **Gracious God, we go forth into this week renewing our commitment to give you time; to practice the means of grace in our families; and to look for you in symbol, word, and deed. Amen.**

Extinguish the candle.

WEEK 2

Preparation for the second practice of the season

OPENING PRAYER (5 MINUTES)

Light the Christ candle.

ADVENT	**We light the candle in anticipation of Jesus' birth, Emmanuel, God-with-Us.**
LENT	**We light the candle as a reminder of God's presence with us on the journey to Easter.**
SUMMER	**We light the candle as a reminder of God's divine spark of creativity.**
BACK TO SCHOOL	**We light the candle as a reminder of God's presence with us wherever we go.**

Then offer a prayer.

ADVENT	**God of Advent, teach us to wait with the same joy, expectancy, and delight as our children. Amen.**
LENT	**God of Resurrection, give us courage to lead our children faithfully during this awkward season of Lent. Amen.**
SUMMER	**God of beauty, inspire us as cocreators of art. Amen.**
BACK TO SCHOOL	**God of love, we long to bear the fruit of your Spirit and see that same fruit in the lives of our children. Amen.**

PRAYER OF EXAMEN (15 MINUTES)

Remind the group that each week will begin by taking time to remember the previous week: the highs and lows, the times when God felt most present and most absent. If it's helpful, follow the prompts and questions from the first week. If not, simply ask the group to take five minutes of silence to remember the week, imagine God walking with them through the past days. After a moment of silence invite a volunteer to tell about a moment of consolation (a connection with God) or desolation (a disconnection from God). *This is not a time to offer suggestions or compare similar situations. Simply share in a safe and supportive group where God is at work in the families gathered.*

OPTIONAL LECTIO DIVINA (15 MINUTES)

This week the group has the option to explore a prayer practice called *lectio divina,* or "divine reading."

If your group has a full hour to gather, I encourage you to lead this process with the group. With less time, focus instead on the Prayer of Examen and preparing for the coming week.

Explain that *lectio divina* is one of the most central and ancient of Christian practices. We begin by reading a few verses of the Bible. We read unhurriedly so that we may listen for the message God has for us there. We stay alert to connections the Spirit may reveal between the passage and what is going on in our lives. We ask, "What are you saying to me today, Lord? What am I to hear in this story, parable, or prophecy?" Listening in this way requires patience and a willingness to let go of our own agendas and open ourselves to God's shaping.

Say, **I will read the scripture three times. The first time I encourage you to listen for a word or phrase that stands out to you. Once you hear it, repeat it in your mind until I have finished the reading. After a moment of silence I will ask each person to tell the group the word or phrase with no explanation.**

The second time I read the scripture, I encourage you to engage all your senses and imagine the scripture playing out like a movie or play. Notice what or who stands out to you, intrigues you in the story. After a moment of silence I will ask each person to tell the group the image or character that captured his or her imagination. Again with no explanation.

The third and last time I read the scripture I encourage you to be in prayer, listening for God's message to you today. How are the word or phrase and the image relevant to your life and your family today? After a moment of silence I will ask each person to tell the group what he or she found meaningful about this scripture.

Advent: Lead *lectio divina* using Matthew 2:1-6
Lent: Lead *lectio divina* using Exodus 34:27-31
Summer: Lead *lectio divina* using 1 Samuel 16:19-23
Back to School: Lead *lectio divina* using Romans 12:9-13

Scripture and Tradition (10 minutes)

Ask participants to turn to the first page of the season where they can see the Practice, Symbol, Scripture, and Prayer on one page.

Advent

Ask a volunteer to read Matthew 2:1-2.

Say, **It seems like most of the advice we give to our children are in the form of warnings because of our fear for their health and safety: Don't eat that. Don't talk to strangers. Don't cross the street without looking both ways. Advent reminds us of light in the darkness and focuses on hope instead of fear.**

Ask a volunteer to read the description of the practice for this week, HOPE.
Discuss how the author chose hope instead of fear in the Introduction to the week.
And ask for volunteers to share an experience of hope fulfilled, a time when light shined when all seemed dark.

Ask a volunteer to read the description of the symbol, the STAR, and read the daily practice.

Invite the group to discuss the reasons it's difficult to hope. What stands in the way? Encourage the participants to tell their stories of hope to their children when they explain the practice for the week.

Finally, pray together the daily prayer, "Dear God, when life seems dark, show me the light of hope. Amen."

Lent

Ask a volunteer to read Exodus 34:28.

Say, **The idea of fasting often brings to mind only feelings of discomfort and annoyance. But those who practice the spiritual discipline of fasting do not focus on what they have given up but the beauty of what God provides to fill that void. Moses neither ate nor drank, but he received the Ten Commandments that still guide us these six thousand years later.**

Ask a volunteer to read the description of the practice for this week, FASTING, and the description of the symbol, the EMPTY PLATE.

Ask the group members to discuss the symbolism of an empty plate, one that has never been filled and one that has been licked clean.

Read the practice for this week; brainstorm ways to help children make the connection.

Finally, pray together the daily prayer, "Dear God, I know that I need you as much as I need food. Amen."

Summer

Ask a volunteer to read 1 Samuel 16:23.

Say, **Music can evoke deep emotions in us, transporting us to another time and place, calming the demons inside us like Saul, or pumping us up before a sporting event.**

Ask a volunteer to read the description of the practice for this week, MUSIC.

Have the group members share the types of music they most enjoy. Do they sing or play instruments? How often do they listen to or play music in or as a family?

Have they ever thought about music as holy? as a way to connect to God? How do they experience that connection?

Ask a volunteer to read the description of the symbol, the LYRE.

Encourage each person to tell his or her children tonight about a favorite song or instrument. Play music tonight while you make dinner or sing a lullaby before bedtime.

Finally, pray together the daily prayer, "Dear God, delight me with music. Amen."

Back to School

Ask a volunteer to read Romans 12:12.

Say, **Patience seems more difficult to find and practice with every passing year. Our culture promises immediate access to information and wants us to believe we can have everything prepared, shipped or e-mailed without delay. But the promises are false and patience is still a virtue.**

Ask a volunteer to read the description of the practice for this week, PATIENCE.

When or where are they most likely to lose their patience? What does it look like?

Do their children experience them as patient? How have they learned or struggled with patience?

Ask a volunteer to read the description of the symbol TURTLE. Encourage the group to talk with their children about the benefits of moving more slowly through life, rather than racing through tasks and conversations. Be prepared to give examples.

Finally, pray together the daily prayer, "Dear God, slow me down enough to teach me wisdom and help me see joy. Amen."

PREPARATION FOR THE WEEK (10 MINUTES)

Ask the participants to form groups of two or three. Encourage people from the same family to remain together. Discuss the following questions:

- What did you enjoy about the daily practice? How was it a struggle?
- How did you choose to check in with your kids each day? What went well? What flopped?
- What is exciting or challenging about the daily prayer and practice this week?

Gather and ask the group for specific ways that the group can pray in the coming week.

CLOSING (5 MINUTES)

Offer a prayer of your own or something like this, **Gracious God, we go forth into this week renewing our commitment to give you time; to practice the means of grace in our families; and to look for you in symbol, word, and deed. Amen.**

Extinguish the candle.

WEEK 3

Preparation for the third practice of the season

This week you will need paper and pens or pencils for each participant if you choose to do the journaling exercise.

OPENING PRAYER (5 MINUTES)

Light the Christ candle.

ADVENT	**We light the candle in anticipation of Jesus' birth, Emmanuel, God-with-Us.**
LENT	**We light the candle as a reminder of God's presence with us on the journey to Easter.**
SUMMER	**We light the candle as a reminder of God's divine spark of creativity.**
BACK TO SCHOOL	**We light the candle as a reminder of God's presence with us wherever we go.**

Then offer a prayer.

ADVENT	**God of Advent, teach us to wait with the same joy, expectancy, and delight as our children. Amen.**
LENT	**God of Resurrection, give us courage to lead our children faithfully during this awkward season of Lent. Amen.**
SUMMER	**God of beauty, inspire us as cocreators of art. Amen.**
BACK TO SCHOOL	**God of love, we long to bear the fruit of your Spirit and see that same fruit in the lives of our children. Amen.**

PRAYER OF EXAMEN (15 MINUTES)

Remind the group that each week will begin by taking time to remember the previous week: the highs and lows, the times when God felt most present and most absent. If it's helpful, follow all the prompts and questions from the first week. If not, simply ask the group to take five minutes of silence to remember the week, imagine God walking with them through the past days. After a moment of silence invite a volunteer to tell about a moment of consolation (a connection with God) or desolation (a disconnection from God). *This is not a time to offer suggestions or compare similar situations. Simply share in a safe and supportive group where God is at work in the families gathered.*

Optional Journaling (15 minutes)

If the group has a full hour to gather, I encourage you to lead this process with the group. With less time you may focus instead on the Prayer of Examen and preparation for the coming week.

This week the group will have time to journal about their experience of daily spiritual practices. Journaling is a gift of our spiritual journey in many ways. First, we know that the Word is eternal—with God from the beginning. With words God spoke the world into being. Words are sacred. Second, the process of putting pen to paper (or typing to the screen) slow us down long enough to reflect and capture our thoughts. And third, it creates a record of our journey. Whether the words never see the light of day or they are shared with a spouse or friend, a question or an insight is captured in time.

Pass out paper and pens to each person.

Say, **Think back to the examen we just completed. Choose one of the moments from this week that you want to spend some more time reflecting on.**

Now fold your paper in half vertically. The left side of the paper is for your words. The right side is for God. You are the scribe for both of you. Begin the conversation with your thoughts, questions, concerns about the moment from the week that you chose.

Take a minute to listen for God's response. Write down whatever comes to you on the right side of the page. This may seem strange or presumptuous but I encourage you to try. I'll give you five to eight minutes.

When everyone has finished, ask for volunteers to share their conversations. They may share comments on the process or specific dialogue from the journaling time.

Scripture and Tradition (10 minutes)

Advent

Ask a volunteer to read Luke 2:19.

Say, **This is a beautiful description of parenting and of our way of praying for our children. With each milestone, scraped knee, squeal of delight, broken heart, and new friend, we capture the moments and hold them in our hearts. We can't always hold or hug on our kids, especially as they become preteens and adolescents, but we can hold them in our heart, puzzling and marveling as they grow and change before our eyes.**

Ask a volunteer to read the description of the practice for this week, PRAYER, and the description of the symbol, the TREASURE CHEST.

Ask participants to discuss the connection they see between prayer and the heart.

Read the practice for this week; brainstorm ways to help children make the connection.

Finally, pray together the daily prayer, "Dear God, listen to all the love and feelings I treasure in my heart. Amen."

Lent

Ask a volunteer to read Luke 12:33.

Say, **During Lent we remember Jesus' life, his compassion and generosity. Reading the Gospels, we cannot deny that following Jesus not only touches our hearts but also changes our attachment to our possessions and our willingness to share what we have.**

Ask members of the group to share honestly their gut reaction to this verse. Does it inspire them or anger them? How do they feel about Jesus making demands on their possessions?

Ask a volunteer to read the description of the practice for this week, CHARITY, and the description of the symbol, the LOAF OF BREAD.

Ask the group members to discuss their children's generosity: a funny story of hoarding cereal or a heartwarming story of a lemonade stand for a good cause.

Do your children know people in need? Where do they see places of abundance in their lives?

Finally, pray together the daily prayer, "Dear God, give me a generous heart. Amen." Say, **By virtue of the fact that you are sitting in this circle, you must believe or have some inclination that attention to God, prayer, and regular worship are important to your family's growth and development. We all struggle, no matter how good our intentions, to commit to daily devotions. This week we remind ourselves and our children that prayer and devotion can happen any time, anywhere.**

Summer

Ask a volunteer to read Exodus 15:20.

Say, **There has been debate through the centuries about the appropriateness of dance in the Christian tradition. But as we read today, dance was a spontaneous and joyful response to God's action and saving power in lives of the Hebrew people. Dancing allows us to use our whole selves—mind *and* body to praise God.**

Ask a volunteer to read the description of the practice for this week, DANCE, and the description of the symbol, the TAMBOURINE.

Ask the group to remember and describe the ways their children dance. When was the first time their child began bouncing or wiggling to the sound of music or a beat? What was he or she feeling? What did it inspire in them?

Has their children and they themselves been able to maintain that spontaneity and love of dance and movement?

Finally, pray together the daily prayer, "Dear God, thank you for fingers and toes and legs and arms that can move and dance. Amen."

Back to School

Ask a volunteer to read Psalm 86:11.

Say, **Often we think of self-control as limiting those things we love or enjoy, like dessert or time spent online. But the psalmist describes self-control as a focus on those things that are most important, the things that bring joy to us and God.**

Ask a volunteer to read the description of the practice for this week, SELF-CONTROL, and the description of the symbol, the YIELD SIGN.

Ask the individuals in the group to discuss which traffic signals and signs best describe the way he or she usually makes decisions—red or green light, SLIPPERY WHEN WET. How would their interactions with their children or coworkers or spouse differ if they imagined a yield sign?

Finally, pray together the daily prayer, "Dear God, when I yield, show me how to live your will. Amen."

PREPARATION FOR THE WEEK (10 MINUTES)

Ask the participants to form groups of two or three. Encourage people from the same family to remain together. Discuss the following questions:

- What did you enjoy about the daily practice? How was it a struggle?

- How did you choose to check in with your kids each day? What went well? What flopped?

- What is exciting or challenging about the daily prayer and practice this week?

Gather and ask the group for specific ways that the group can pray in the coming week.

CLOSING (5 MINUTES)

Offer a prayer of your own or something like this, "Gracious God, we go forth into this week renewing our commitment to give you time; to practice the means of grace in our families; and to look for you in symbol, word, and deed. Amen."

Extinguish the candle.

WEEK 4

Preparation for the fourth practice of the season

OPENING PRAYER (5 MINUTES)

Light the Christ candle.

ADVENT	**We light the candle in anticipation of Jesus' birth, Emmanuel, God-with-Us.**
LENT	**We light the candle as a reminder of God's presence with us on the journey to Easter.**
SUMMER	**We light the candle as a reminder of God's divine spark of creativity.**
BACK TO SCHOOL	**We light the candle as a reminder of God's presence with us wherever we go.**

Then offer a prayer.

ADVENT	**God of Advent, teach us to wait with the same joy, expectancy, and delight as our children. Amen.**
LENT	**God of Resurrection, give us courage to lead our children faithfully during this awkward season of Lent. Amen.**
SUMMER	**God of beauty, inspire us as cocreators of art. Amen**
BACK TO SCHOOL	**God of love, we long to bear the fruit of your Spirit and see that same fruit in the lives of our children. Amen.**

PRAYER OF EXAMEN (15 MINUTES)

Remind the group that each week will begin by taking time to remember the previous week: the highs and lows, the times when God felt most present and most absent. If its helpful, follow all the prompts and questions from the first week. If not, simply ask the group to take five minutes of silence to remember the week, imagine God walking with them through the past days. After a moment of silence invite a volunteer to tell about a moment of consolation (a connection with God) or desolation (a disconnection from God). *This is not a time to offer suggestions or compare similar situations. Simply share in a safe and supportive group where God is at work in the families gathered.*

OPTIONAL HOLY LISTENING (15 MINUTES)

If your group has a full hour to gather, I encourage you to lead this process. With less time you may focus instead on the Prayer of Examen and preparing for the coming week.

This week the group will have the opportunity to practice Holy Listening. Deeply listening to one another without distraction or agenda is a gift in our world of constant sound and competition. This exercise is difficult for the listener but can also be equally, if not more, vulnerable for the speaker who may experience the gift of silence and being heard for the first time in a long time.

Say, **Think back to the examen we just completed. Choose one of the moments from this week that you want to spend some more time reflecting on. Form groups of two, and talk about that moment. You can choose to be with your partner or not.**

Holy Listening means providing a sacred space for persons to speak their joys and fears without rushing, without judgment and without providing a defense. In the moments that follow, each person will have five minutes to be the Speaker and be listened to deeply. Listener, you *only* listen. You don't ask questions. You don't offer a similar story. You don't correct or offer advice. You may offer encouraging words or sounds like, "yes" or "mmm hmm." But other than that, you simply listen.

After five minutes we will switch and allow the Listener to be the Speaker. Begin.

After each person has had a chance to speak, invite persons to comment on the process and what it felt like to be both the Speaker and the Listener.

Scripture and Tradition (10 minutes)

Advent

Ask a volunteer to read Luke 2:21-35.

Say, **Those of you who have gathered for a class of this nature understand the gift and strength of raising our children in a community. But so much in our world teaches us that we should be strong on our own, that depending on others signals weakness or failure.**

Ask the group members if they have considered the community that surrounded and supported Jesus. How have they experienced the church as a community for their children?

Ask a volunteer to read the description of the practice for this week, COMMUNITY OF FAITH, and the description of the symbol, the CIRCLE OF FRIENDS.

Ask the group members to discuss the ways they have experienced the strength of community. Who provides community for their children? Discuss ways they can help their children see this week the many people who surround and support them.

Finally, pray together the daily prayer, "Dear God, I am grateful for my circle of friends who love You. Amen."

Lent

Ask a volunteer to read the description of the practice for this week, DEVOTION.

Discuss your attempts at daily devotion. What did it look like—reading the Bible? journaling? Centering Prayer? What were the challenges and the benefits?

What can be a daily prompt or cue for them to remember to give thanks to God?

Ask a volunteer to read the description of the symbol, the PALM BRANCH, and read the daily practice.

Encourage each person to tell his or her children tonight what time or cue will prompt them to praise God each day this week.

Finally, pray together the daily prayer, "Dear God, I am grateful and I need your help. Amen."

Summer

Ask a volunteer to read Jeremiah 30:2.

Say, **Our Bible itself may be the greatest testimony to the value and beauty of writing. The Gospel of John even describes Jesus as the Word, "the Word was with God, and the Word was God" (John 1:1). Writing can express beauty and capture tales of beauty that we can share with one another.**

Ask the group to discuss how writing can be creative. How do the members believe God works to inspire great writings like scripture or classic novels or our personal journal entries? Have they found writing to be a way of prayer?

Ask a volunteer to read the description of the practice for this week, WRITING, and the description of the symbol, the PEN.

Some of their children may just be learning to hold a crayon while others have already written term papers. Do their children enjoy writing? With increasing technology, how often do their children pick up crayon or pen to write or draw on paper? Is this good or bad?

Finally, pray together the daily prayer, "Dear God, thank you for all the people who have written so that I can know and learn. Amen."

Back to School

Ask a volunteer to read Ephesians 4:32.

Say, **Often when we remember the people who made the biggest impact on our lives it is precisely because of their simple acts of kindness in our lives—a word of encouragement, an invitation to coffee at the right time, the gift of a book. We long for our children to know and offer these same kindnesses.**

Ask the group to discuss how easy or difficult it is to accept someone else's kindness without returning the favor.

Ask a volunteer to read the description of the practice for this week, KINDNESS, and the description of the symbol, the SUNFLOWER. The sunflower is a tall, bright, and beautiful reminder of God's goodness. What other flowers, plants, or objects remind you of kindness and grace?

Finally, pray together the daily prayer, "Dear God, let my kindness shine like a sunflower. Amen."

PREPARATION FOR THE WEEK (10 MINUTES)

Ask the participants to form groups of two or three. Encourage people from the same family to remain together. Discuss the following questions:

- How has your understanding of spiritual practices changed over these few weeks?

- What patterns do you hope to create and maintain in your family?

- What about the daily prayer and practice excites or challenges you this week?

Gather and ask the group for specific ways that the group can pray in the coming week.

CLOSING (5 MINUTES)

Offer a prayer of your own or something like this, **Gracious God, we go forth into this week renewing our commitment to give you time; to practice the means of grace in our families; and to look for you in symbol, word and deed. Amen.**

Extinguish the candle.

Optional Sessions

I wrote this book assuming four weeks as a realistic amount of time for individual families and groups of families to organize, maintain a pattern, and coordinate schedules. So I have provided four weeks in four separate seasons of the year. But I wanted to provide some additional material to create flexible and additional options. If your family enjoys the first four-week season that you participate in—the practice, family gathering, and time committed to spiritual formation—and doesn't want to take a break, then continue on, using the additional weeks provided here.

Many Sunday school classes and small groups may desire a six-week series. If you prefer a longer season, I provide two additional weeks for each of the four seasons. There is no corresponding material for the Leader's Guide but I trust that you will have settled into the pattern and adapted it to make it work for your group for these additional weeks. I have labeled the additional eight practices to correspond to the four exisiting seasons. But you could also use them to create two additional stand-alone seasons of four weeks each.

While the practices described in the book tie nicely to each season, each one is a traditional spiritual practice that your family can explore any time during the year. Feel free to browse the practices that best complement the ways God is moving and prompting you as a family. I hope you will enjoy these additional weeks, incorporate them in creative ways, and, above all, find your family formed daily in the image of Christ.

Advent (Option 1): Peace

PEACE: "A state of tranquility and quiet." An individual and a community can experience peace.

The DOVE, since the story of Noah saved from the Flood, has represented the end of trial, the reconciliation and salvation of persons and a community.

Read Romans 15:13.
May the God of hope fill you with all joy and peace as you trust in him.

Daily Practice

This week try to be a peacemaker.

Toddler	Every time you see a bird in the sky, imagine you are flying and peaceful.
Elementary	When you are sad this week or you see someone who is upset, imagine a dove bringing just the right thing to make you or the other person feel better.
Junior & Senior High	Peace comes when we trust God for the answers that we can't see. When you are tempted to shout, use kind words. When you are tempted to slam doors, say how you feel. When you are tempted to ignore, ask a question. Notice how peace changes relationships.
Adult	This week consciously demonstrate peaceful resolutions to problems. What olive branch can you offer to your boss? your spouse? How can you help your children seek peace instead of separating them or punishing them?

Daily Prayer

You may post this prayer on your door, the refrigerator, your dashboard, or on the dining room table. Pray the prayer throughout the day, individually and together.

Dear God, be near to me this week like a gentle dove. Amen.

FAMILY GATHERING

(after practicing a week of Peace)

OPENING

Dear God, this week we tried to bring peace into our lives and the world. Thank you for . . . [each person can offer thanks for pets, people, answered prayers, weather, events, grades, safety, birthdays, and so on.]

THE WORD

Don't be anxious about anything; rather bring up all of your requests to God in your prayers and petitions, along with giving thanks. Then the peace of God that exceeds all understanding will keep your hearts and minds safe in Christ Jesus (Phil. 4:6-7).

RESPONSE

Draw or write a word, phrase, or prayer about practicing peace: a learning, something to remember, an "aha" moment, an answered prayer.

LOOKING FORWARD

Look together at next week's scripture and daily practice. Ask questions and talk about ways to incorporate the practice into your week.

PRAYER

Dear God, today we pray for . . . [each person can name people, situations, events, concerns that he or she needs prayer for this week].

Pray together the Lord's Prayer.

Advent (Option 2): Faithfulness

FAITHFULNESS: "Having or showing true and constant affection or loyalty."

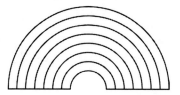

The RAINBOW is an ancient reminder of God's love and faithfulness to God's promises.

Read Genesis 9:16-17.

> **The bow will be in the clouds, and upon seeing it I will remember the enduring covenant between God and every living being of all the earth's creatures. God said to Noah, "This is the symbol of the covenant that I have set up between me and all creatures on earth."**

DAILY PRACTICE

Keep promises and show consistent love to family and friends.

Toddler & Elementary	When you make a promise or say "I love you" this week, draw a rainbow with the tip of your finger to remind yourself to be faithful.
Junior & Senior High	After the flood in Genesis (chapters 6–9), God put a rainbow in the sky as a reminder of God's promise not to destroy all life again (Gen. 9:17). We all need symbols to remind us of our promises. How have you promised to be faithful? With a verbal promise, a handshake, exchange of money? Honor those promises this week.
Adult	In any given week we make verbal promises to our spouse, children, or boss. We sign consent forms at doctors' offices and click agreements on websites. We make vows in marriage, baptism, and confirmation. In what public ways do we remind ourselves of those promises? Tell your kids of one way you have been faithful and the ways God has been faithful to you.

DAILY PRAYER

You may post this prayer on your door, the refrigerator, your dashboard, or on the dining room table. Pray the prayer throughout the day, individually and together.

Dear God, thank you for your faithfulness. Help me to be faithful. Amen.

FAMILY GATHERING

(after practicing a week of Faithfulness)

OPENING

Dear God, this week we tried to be faithful as you are faithful. Thank you for . . . [each person can offer thanks for pets, people, answered prayers, weather, events, grades, safety, birthdays, and so on.]

THE WORD

Know now then that the LORD your God is the only true God! He is the faithful God, who keeps the covenant and proves loyal to everyone who loves him and keeps his commands—even to the thousandth generation! (Deut. 7:9).

RESPONSE

Draw or write a word, phrase, prayer about practicing faithfulness: a learning, something to remember, an "aha" moment, an answered prayer.

LOOKING FORWARD

Look together at next week's scripture and daily practice. Ask questions and talk about ways to incorporate the practice into your week.

PRAYER

Dear God, today we pray for . . . [each person can name people, situations, events, concerns that he or she needs prayer for this week].

Pray together the Lord's Prayer.

Lent (Option 1): Silence

SILENCE: "Absence of sound or noise."

The EMPTY THOUGHT BUBBLE reminds us that sometimes we need to stop talking, even in prayer, and listen—especially for God.

Read Psalm 62:5.

Oh, I must find rest in God only because my hope comes from him!

Daily Practice

Listen for God in the silence.

Toddler	When you are in your bedroom, try to be absolutely quiet. Listen for God.
Elementary	Do you ever hear silence? Find a time and place today to be in silence. Listen for God.
Junior & Senior High	Silence is rare. In today's world we need to create silence. Find a place every day to create silence and listen for God.
Adult	Silence can feel uncomfortable at first. Practice silence by yourself, and then choose a few minutes (as long as your family can tolerate) in your home when everyone is silent. Listen for God.

Daily Prayer

You may post this prayer on your door, the refrigerator, your dashboard, or on the dining room table. Say the prayer throughout the day, individually and together.

Dear God, we want to hear you instead of the noise of the world. Amen.

FAMILY GATHERING

(after practicing a week of Silence)

OPENING

Dear God, it is difficult to hear you when the world is so loud. We will try to be quiet and listen for you. Thank you for . . . [each person can offer thanks for pets, people, answered prayers, weather, events, grades, safety, birthdays, and so on.]

THE WORD

So faith comes from listening, but it's listening by means of Christ's message (Rom. 10:17).

RESPONSE

Draw or write a word, phrase, prayer about practicing silence: a learning, something to remember, an "aha" moment, an answered prayer.

LOOKING FORWARD

Look together at next week's scripture and daily practice. Ask questions and talk about ways to incorporate the practice into your week.

PRAYER

Dear God, today we pray for . . . [each person can name people, situations, events, concerns that he or she needs prayer for this week].

Pray together the Lord's Prayer.

Lent (Option 2): Alms

ALMS: "Something given freely to relieve the poor." We can be generous, or charitable, with all of our possessions. Alms refers specifically to how we offer our money.

The COIN reminds us that God wants us to share what we have with those who have less.

Read 1 Timothy 6:18.

Tell them to do good, to be rich in the good things they do, to be generous, and to share with others.

DAILY PRACTICE

Give an offering of money this week to your church or an organization your family supports.

Toddler	Collect coins this week, and put them in a bowl or jar. Give them to someone who needs money.
Elementary	Have you ever received money? What did it feel like? Choose a way that you can share your money this week.
Junior & Senior High	If you receive an allowance, have a job, or receive money as a gift, decide this week to give a percentage of it to someone or to an organization you feel passionate about.
Adult	If you contribute to your church or charities, tell your children about it. Why do you give? How did you choose that organization? What special need in your community could your family donate to?

DAILY PRAYER

You may post this prayer on your door, the refrigerator, your dashboard, or on the dining room table. Say the prayer throughout the day, individually and together.

Dear God, this week we want to share what we have. Amen.

FAMILY GATHERING

(after practicing a week of Alms)

OPENING

Dear God, we want to become more generous and give with joy. We will try to be quiet and listen for you. Thank you for . . . [each person can offer thanks for pets, people, answered prayers, weather, events, grades, safety, birthdays, and so on.]

THE WORD

Everyone should give whatever they have decided in their heart. They shouldn't give with hesitation or because of pressure. God loves a cheerful giver (2 Cor. 9:7).

RESPONSE

Draw or write a word, phrase, prayer about practicing alms: a learning, something to remember, an "aha" moment, an answered prayer.

LOOKING FORWARD

Look together at next week's scripture and daily practice. Ask questions and talk about ways to incorporate the practice into your week.

PRAYER

Dear God, today we pray for . . . [each person can name people, situations, events, concerns that he or she needs prayer for this week].

Pray together The Lord's Prayer.

SUMMER (OPTION 1): CREATIVITY

CREATIVITY: "Bringing something new or original into being."

CLAY reminds us that God created the world from nothing, and it was good.

Read Amos 4:13.

> **The one who forms the mountains, creates the wind, makes known his thoughts to humankind, makes the morning darkness and moves over the heights of the earth—the LORD, the God of heavenly forces is his name!**

DAILY PRACTICE

Make, try, and affirm new things.

Toddler	Clap every time you try something new or see something new.
Elementary	Create or try something new every day, in private or in public.
Junior & Senior High	School is out; testing is over for now. Try something new, and find a way to compliment someone for trying something new too.
Adult	Take time out of your day to create something new—a meal you've never tried, a birdhouse for the yard, or write a poem. And encourage your family members to try something new.

DAILY PRAYER

You may post this prayer on your door, the refrigerator, your dashboard, or on the dining room table. Say the prayer throughout the day, individually and together.

Dear God, this week I want to cocreate with you. Amen.

FAMILY GATHERING

(after practicing a week of Creativity)

OPENING

Dear God, this week we tried to be open to trying new things and putting to use new skills. Thank you for . . . [each person can offer thanks for pets, people, answered prayers, weather, events, grades, safety, birthdays, and so on.]

THE WORD

The wise hear them and grow in wisdom; those with understanding gain guidance (Prov. 1:5).

RESPONSE

Draw or write a word, phrase, prayer about practicing creativity: a learning, something to remember, an "aha" moment, an answered prayer.

LOOKING FORWARD

Look together at next week's scripture and daily practice. Ask questions and talk about ways to incorporate the practice into your week.

PRAYER

Dear God, today we pray for . . . [each person can name people, situations, events, concerns that he or she needs prayer for this week].

Pray together the Lord's Prayer.

SUMMER (OPTION 2): STORYTELLING

STORYTELLING: "Reciting tales or anecdotes."

A CANDLE reminds us of parents and children, friends and neighbors who have gathered in the evenings for centuries to hear the stories of faith and family and tradition.

Read John 1:1-2.

In the beginning was the Word and the Word was with God and the Word was God. The Word was with God in the beginning.

DAILY PRACTICE

Tell a story or ask to hear a story.

Toddler	Tell a story to someone today.
Elementary	Tell someone a story today about something that happened to you that you will never forget. Ask someone to tell you a story about something he or she will never forget.
Junior & Senior High	Tell someone a story that explains what you know or what you wonder about God. Ask someone to tell you a story that explains who God is or how God acts.
Adult	Stories are a way to share our wisdom, insights, and morals without repeating the same rules over and over. Tell your children a story that helps explain your understanding of God or your hope for them.

DAILY PRAYER

You may post this prayer on your door, the refrigerator, your dashboard, or on the dining room table. Say the prayer throughout the day, individually and together.

Dear God, I want to have the patience to tell and listen to stories. Amen.

FAMILY GATHERING

(after practicing a week of Storytelling)

OPENING

Dear God, we are thankful the stories we hear and for writing the story of our lives. Thank you for . . . [each person can offer thanks for pets, people, answered prayers, weather, events, grades, safety, birthdays, and so on.]

THE WORD

Now, after having investigated everything carefully from the beginning, I have also decided to write a carefully ordered account for you, most honorable Theophilus. I want you to have confidence in the soundness of the instruction you have received (Luke 1:3-4).

RESPONSE

Draw or write a word, phrase, prayer about practicing storytelling: a learning, something to remember, an "aha" moment, an answered prayer.

LOOKING FORWARD

Look together at next week's scripture and daily practice. Ask questions and talk about ways to incorporate the practice into your week.

PRAYER

Dear God, today we pray for . . . [each person can name people, situations, events, concerns that he or she needs prayer for this week].

Pray together the Lord's Prayer.

BACK TO SCHOOL (OPTION 1): GENTLENESS

GENTLENESS: "Mildness of manners and self-control."

The ELEPHANT reminds us that a creature can have great strength while moving in the world with gentleness.

Read Philippians 4:5.

Let your gentleness show in your treatment of all people. The Lord is near.

DAILY PRACTICE

Move as gently as you can through your days, leaving a place or person calmer than when you entered.

Toddler & Elementary	Did you know the bottom of an elephant's foot feels like a pencil eraser? Soft and rubbery. Imagine your strong and wiggly body walking through your house and classroom this week with feet as soft as pencil erasers.
Junior & Senior High	An elephant's trunk has more than 40,000 individual muscles, and it is strong enough to uproot trees and carry logs. But it is also sensitive and gentle enough to pick leaves from the tip of a branch. How can you use your great strengths in gentle ways this week? Smart enough to tutor someone else? Strong enough to help your elderly neighbor rake leaves? Sensitive enough to listen to a friend without judging?
Adult	As parents and adults we have so much power to control our children's lives and boundaries, to correct and shame. How can you parent this week with grace, forgiveness, and gentleness?

DAILY PRAYER

You may post this prayer on your door, the refrigerator, your dashboard, or on the dining room table. Say the prayer throughout the day, individually and together.

Dear God, teach me to be strong and gentle at the same time. Amen.

FAMILY GATHERING

(after practicing a week of Gentleness)

OPENING

Dear God, this week we learned that we can be strong and gentle at the same time. Thank you for . . . [each person can offer thanks for pets, people, answered prayers, weather, events, grades, safety, birthdays, and so on.]

THE WORD

A sensitive answer turns back wrath, but an offensive word stirs up anger (Prov. 15:1).

RESPONSE

Draw or write a word, phrase, prayer about practicing gentleness: a learning, something to remember, an "aha" moment, an answered prayer.

LOOKING FORWARD

Look together at next week's scripture and daily practice. Ask questions and talk about ways to incorporate the practice into your week.

PRAYER

Dear God, today we pray for . . . [each person can name people, situations, events, concerns that he or she needs prayer for this week].

Pray together the Lord's Prayer.

BACK TO SCHOOL (OPTION 2): GOODNESS

GOODNESS: A deliberate choice for what has quality; for what is right, generous, and kind.

The light of the SUN touches every thing on earth and reminds us that everything that God created is good.

Read Timothy 4:4.

> **Everything that has been created by God is good, and nothing that is received with thanksgiving should be rejected.**

DAILY PRACTICE

In the story of creation in Genesis, God blesses each day of creation by calling it "good." See the good in the world each day this week.

Toddler & Elementary	Every time you see, taste, hear, touch, or smell something you like, say, "Thank you, God, it is good."
Junior & Senior High	Each day name something that you think is good: a delicious meal, a beautiful photo, a nice person. Then decide how you can multiply that goodness. Make that meal for your family; post the photo on social media or take one of your own; write a thank-you note to the kind person.
Adult	Goodness often goes unnoticed and uncelebrated or is overshadowed by the bad in the world. This week tell your kids about the good you see in the world, in your family, in them: a simple sentence about the beauty of the sunset, a word of appreciation for sharing with a sibling, a quick phone call to grandma to say I love you, or telling a story at dinner about a kindness you read in the paper.

DAILY PRAYER

You may post this prayer on your door, the refrigerator, your dashboard, or on the dining room table. Say the prayer throughout the day, individually and together.

> ***Dear God, show me the goodness that is all around me. Amen.***

FAMILY GATHERING

(after practicing a week of Goodness)

OPENING

Dear God, this week we looked for the good in our daily lives. Thank you for . . . [each person can offer thanks for pets, people, answered prayers, weather, events, grades, safety, birthdays, and so on.]

THE WORD

The Lord is good to everyone and everything; God's compassion extends to all his handiwork! (Ps. 145:9).

RESPONSE

Draw or write a word, phrase, prayer about practicing goodness: a learning, something to remember, an "aha" moment, an answered prayer.

LOOKING FORWARD

Look together at next week's scripture and daily practice. Ask questions and talk about ways to incorporate the practice into your week.

PRAYER

Dear God, today we pray for . . . [each person can name people, situations, events, concerns that he or she needs prayer for this week].

Pray together the Lord's Prayer.

About the Author

Kara Lassen Oliver works part-time for Discipleship Ministries of The United Methodist Church. She trains and equips authors in Africa to tell the stories of God at work in the world. She is also a freelance editor and author. Living two years in Malawi, Africa, with her family members as United Methodist Volunteers in Mission opened her eyes to the beauty of life that is often simultaneously joy-filled and painful. Kara has a master of divinity from Vanderbilt Divinity School but finds that marriage and parenting teach her the most about love and justice, compassion and mercy.

CPSIA information can be obtained
at www.ICGtesting.com
Printed in the USA
FSOW02n1025040316
17620FS

9 780835 814973